It's another Quality Book from CGP

This book is for anyone doing GCSE Maths at
Foundation Level, with a predicted grade of D or below.
(If you're not sure what your predicted grade is, your teacher will be able to tell you.)

All the important topics are explained in a clear, straightforward
way to help you get all the marks you can in the exam.

And of course, there are some daft bits to make
the whole thing vaguely entertaining for you.

What CGP is all about

Our sole aim here at CGP is to produce the highest quality
books — carefully written, immaculately presented and
dangerously close to being funny.

Then we work our socks off to get them out to you
— at the cheapest possible prices.

Published by CGP

Written by Richard Parsons

Updated by: Helena Hayes, Janet West, Dawn Wright.

With thanks to Katherine Craig and Ann Francis for the proofreading.

ISBN: 978 1 84762 645 5

Groovy website: www.cgpbooks.co.uk
Printed by Elanders Ltd, Newcastle upon Tyne.
Jolly bits of clipart from CorelDRAW®

Photocopying — it's dull, grey and sometimes a bit naughty. Luckily, it's dead cheap, easy and quick to
order more copies of this book from CGP — just call us on 0870 750 1242. Phew!

Contents

Calculating Tips

Ah, the wonderful world of <u>GCSE Maths</u>. OK — maybe it's more like smelly socks at times.
GCSE Maths is tested by two or three <u>exams</u> — yuk. Here are some <u>tricks</u> you only
have to learn once, but could get you marks in all your exams. <u>Read on</u>...

Exam marks you say?
I might be able to get
my hands on some.
Meet me by the sewers
at sunset. Come alone.

Don't Be Scared of <u>Wordy Questions</u>

For the 'real-life' questions you've first got to work out
what the question's <u>asking you to do</u>.

> 1) <u>READ</u> the question <u>carefully</u>.
>   Think <u>what bit of maths</u> you might need to answer it.
>
> 2) <u>Underline</u> the <u>BITS YOU NEED</u> to answer the question
>   — you might not have to use <u>all</u> the numbers they give you.
>
> 3) Write out the question <u>IN MATHS</u> and answer it,
>   showing all your <u>working</u> clearly.

Example:
A return car journey from Carlisle to Manchester uses $\frac{4}{7}$ of a tank of petrol.
It costs £56 for a <u>full tank</u> of petrol.
How much does the journey cost?

It doesn't matter where they're driving from and to.

1) The "$\frac{4}{7}$" tells you it's a <u>fractions</u> question.

2) Underline <u>£56</u> (the cost of a full tank) and $\frac{4}{7}$ (the fraction of the tank used).

3) You want to know $\frac{4}{7}$ of £56, so in maths:
$$\frac{4}{7} \times £56 = £32$$

Don't forget the units — this is a question about <u>cost in pounds</u>, so the units will be £.

Fractions questions are covered on page 18.

Don't <u>Reach Straight for the Calculator</u>

You really need to get used to <u>WRITING DOWN YOUR WORKING OUT</u>.

Look at these two answers to this question:
"Find the area of the triangle on the right [3 marks]."

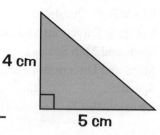

4 cm

5 cm

ANSWER 1: ~~20~~ **✗**

<u>ANSWER 1</u> gets <u>NO MARKS</u> —
20 is wrong and there's
nothing else to give marks for.

ANSWER 2: $A = \frac{1}{2} \times B \times H$ ✓
$= \frac{1}{2} \times 5 \times 4$ ✓
$= 20 \text{ cm}^2$ **✗**

<u>ANSWER 2</u> gets <u>2 MARKS</u> —
so even though the answer's wrong
it still gets most of the marks!

See page 29 for how to
find the area of a triangle.

Calculating Tips

BODMAS

Brackets, **O**ther, **D**ivision, **M**ultiplication, **A**ddition, **S**ubtraction

BODMAS tells you the ORDER in which things should be done in a question:
Work out the bits in Brackets first, then Other things like squaring,
then Divide / Multiply groups of numbers before Adding or Subtracting them.

Example: Work out: $(7 - 4)^2 + 4 \times 3 \div 2$

Work it out in stages :
$= 3^2 + 4 \times 3 \div 2$ • Brackets first
$= 9 + 4 \times 3 \div 2$ • Other (squared)
$= 9 + 6$ • Multiply and Divide
$= 15$ • Add and Subtract

Calculators

You're allowed to use a calculator in some of your exams — hurray!
Make sure you know how your shiny grey friend can help you.

SHIFT (OR 2ND FUNC)

Press this first if you want
to use something written
ABOVE a button
(e.g. the pi (π) button).

THE ANSWER

Before you jot down 3.6,
think about what it means.
E.g. in a money question,
it might mean £3.60.

FRACTIONS

E.g. for $\frac{1}{4}$ press `1` `a b/c` `4`
For $1\frac{3}{5}$ press `1` `a b/c` `3` `a b/c` `5`.

To cancel down a fraction,
enter it and press `=`.

(If you have a button that looks like
`▭/▭` instead, use it in the same way.)

Pressing the `a b/c` or `s↔d` button
also switches an answer
between a fraction and a decimal.

SQUARE, CUBE AND ROOTS

E.g. `4` `x²` gives 4 squared = 16.
And `³√` `27` gives the
cube root of 27 = 3.

(See pages 85-87.)

BRACKETS

Calculators use BODMAS (see above),
so if there's part of a question you
want the calculator to do FIRST then
put brackets in to tell it so.

MEMORY (STO, RCL & M+)

E.g. for $\frac{840}{15 + 12 \times 8}$:

Press `15` `+` `12` `×` `8` `=`
and then `STO` `M+` to store the
bottom line in the memory.

Then press `840` `÷` `RCL` `M+` `=`.
and the answer is 7.57.

The 'Ans' button saves the number you got
when you last pressed the '=' button, so you
can use it like the memory buttons.

PI (π) (See page 30.)

The calculator stores the number
for pi (= 3.142...). If it's above
another button as shown here,
press the `shift` button first.

Calculating Tips

Calculating Tips

Money

You deal with money A LOT in real life — and you get exam questions about it. The main things to watch out for are units (pounds and pence) and decimal places.

Example: Jennie puts £60 into a savings account which pays 1% interest at the end of a year. How much interest does she earn at the end of the year in a) pounds, and b) pence?

1) This percentages question is asking you to find 1% of £60.

2) In maths speak this means: $\frac{1}{100} \times £60 = 0.6$. (See page 20.)
The important bit now is working out what 0.6 means.

> You might have to round things too. E.g. £0.729 would be rounded to £0.73 so there are only 2 decimal places.

3) The question uses pounds (£60), so 0.6 means 0.6 pounds. But answers in pounds should ALWAYS be given to TWO DECIMAL PLACES. This might mean filling the 2nd decimal place with a zero, like this: £0.60.

4) Part b) asks for the answer in pence.
£1 = 100p, so to change pounds into pence we TIMES BY 100: (See page 9.)
$$0.60 \times 100 = 60p$$

5) So the answers are a) £0.60, and b) 60p.

There's more on how to add and subtract with money on page 8.

Using Timetables

Knowing what bus to catch to get somewhere on time is a pretty important skill, and you might even be tested on it in the exam.

Example: Look at the timetable below. What is the time of the latest bus leaving the bus station that would get you to the train station for 7.30 pm?

Bus Timetable				
Bus Station	1845	1900	1915	1930
Market Street	1852	1907	1922	1937
Long Lane Shops	1901	1916	1931	1946
Train Station	1911	1926	1941	1956
Hospital	1923	1938	1953	2008

1) First work out the time you need to be at the train station in 24 hour clock. To find a 'pm' time in 24 hour clock, ADD 12 HOURS:
$$7.30 + 12.00 = 19.30 \text{ (or } 1930\text{)}.$$
Sometimes the dot is left out.

2) Look across the row for the train station times — 1911, 1926, 1941 and 1956. The last two are too late, so the latest one to arrive on time, before 1930, is 1926.

3) Look up that column until you get to the bus station row, and read off the time that bus leaves the bus station — 1900.

> There's more about time on page 38.

4) So the latest bus you could catch leaves the bus station at 1900.

5) To work out the 12 hour clock time, TAKE AWAY 12 HOURS: 19.00 – 12.00 = 7.00 pm.

Learn these three pages, store, then recall...

Learn this stuff — it can really help you whichever exam you're doing. Right then, on with the rest of the show. Ladies and gentlemen — I give you, the one, the only — Maths G C S Eeee.

Ordering Numbers

Here's a cracking page to get you going. You need to be able to:
1) <u>Read big numbers</u> 2) <u>Write them down</u> 3) Put them in <u>order of size</u>.

Split Big Numbers Into Columns and Parts

1) First, you really need to know the <u>names</u> of all the <u>columns</u>. E.g. for the number <u>2 351 243</u>:

<h1 style="text-align:center">2 3 5 1 2 4 3</h1>

2	3	5	1	2	4	3
MILLIONS	HUNDRED-THOUSANDS	TEN-THOUSANDS	THOUSANDS	HUNDREDS	TENS	UNITS

These are the names of the columns.

2) You can then <u>split any number up</u> into its <u>parts</u>, like this:

2 000 000	Two million
300 000	Three hundred thousand
50 000	Fifty thousand
1 000	One thousand
200	Two hundred
40	Four tens (forty)
3	Three units

Line up the columns so you can read the numbers clearly.

→ These add together to make <u>2 351 243</u> again.

Look at Big Numbers in Groups of Three

To <u>read</u> or <u>write</u> a <u>BIG</u> number, follow these <u>steps</u>:

1) Start from the <u>right-hand side</u> of the number →

2) Moving <u>left</u>, ←, put a space <u>every 3 digits</u> to break it up into <u>groups of 3</u>.

3) Now going <u>right</u>, →, <u>read each group of three</u> as a separate number, as shown.

<u>2 351 243</u>

<u>MILLIONS</u> <u>THOUSANDS</u> The rest

So read as: 2 million, 351 thousand, 243
or write fully in words:
Two million, three hundred and fifty-one thousand,
two hundred and forty-three.

Putting Numbers in Order of Size

<u>EXAMPLE</u>: Put the following in order from <u>smallest to biggest</u>:

623   32   486   4563   75   4143

① First put them into <u>groups</u>, the ones with <u>fewest digits</u> first:

A <u>digit</u> is a number 0-9 which sits in a column of a bigger number. E.g. in 623, the digits are 6, 2 and 3.

SMALLER

32	623	4563
75	486	4143

BIGGER

all the 2-digit ones   all the 3-digit ones   all the 4-digit ones

② Then put <u>each group</u> in order of size by <u>comparing the columns left to right</u>:

3 is smaller than 7.

32
75

4 is smaller than 6.

486
623

The 1st digits are the same so look at the 2nd ones — 1 is smaller than 5.

4143
4563

<u>ANSWER</u>:   32   75   486   623   4143   4563

Ordering Numbers

You also need to be able to put <u>decimal numbers</u> in order too. Again, it's all about the columns.
<u>After the decimal point</u> the columns are called <u>decimal places</u>.

Split Decimals Into Decimal Places

1) The <u>decimal places</u> have <u>names</u> too. E.g. for the number <u>41.602</u>:

$$4 \quad 1 \quad . \quad 6 \quad 0 \quad 2$$

TENS   UNITS   DECIMAL   TENTHS   HUNDREDTHS   THOUSANDTHS
POINT

2) You can <u>split up decimals</u> into <u>parts</u> too:

40.000	Four tens (forty)	
1.000	One unit	
0.600	Six tenths	
0.000	Zero hundredths	
0.002	Two thousandths	

With decimals, line up the <u>decimal points</u>.

→ These add together to make <u>41.602</u> again.

Putting Decimals in Order of Size

<u>EXAMPLE</u>: Put the following in order from <u>smallest to biggest</u>:
2.4 0.004 0.0024 0.024 0.04 0.24 4

① For decimals, do the <u>whole-number bit</u> first <u>before</u> looking at the decimal bit.
The numbers <u>2.4</u> and <u>4</u> have <u>whole</u> numbers, so these <u>must be bigger</u> than the rest.

② Now <u>group</u> the numbers that are left by the <u>number of 0s</u> STRAIGHT AFTER THE POINT.
The group with the <u>most 0s comes first</u>, just like this:

SMALLER
| 0.004 |
| 0.0024 |

two 0s

| 0.024 |
| 0.04 |

one 0

| 0.24 |

no 0s

BIGGER

③ Once they're in groups, order them by comparing the <u>decimal places left to right</u>.

2 is smaller than 4.
| 0.0024 |
| 0.004 |

2 is smaller than 4.
| 0.024 |
| 0.04 |

| 0.24 |

Don't forget to put your bigger numbers back in the list.

<u>ANSWER</u>: 0.0024 0.004 0.024 0.04 0.24 2.4 4

Don't call numbers big or small to their face — it's rude...

Putting numbers into order of size isn't too tricky — if you <u>learn the tips</u> on the last two pages.
1) Write these numbers in words: a) 1 234 531   b) 23 456   c) 2415   d) 3402   e) 203 412
2) Write this down as a number: Fifty-six thousand, four hundred and twenty-one
3) Put these numbers in order of size (smallest to biggest): 23 493 87 1029 3004 345 9
4) Put these decimals in order of size (smallest to biggest): 0.37 0.008 0.307 0.1 0.09 0.2

Addition and Subtraction

For your <u>non-calculator exam</u>, you need to know how to do sums with just a <u>pen and paper</u>.

Adding

E.g. Add together 292, 484 and 29

1) Line up the <u>units columns</u> of each number.

2) Add up the columns from <u>right to left</u> starting with the <u>units</u>: $2 + 4 + 9 = \underline{15}$.

   Write the '5' at the <u>bottom</u> of the units column and <u>carry over</u> the '1' to the next column along.

3) Add up the <u>next column</u>, including anything <u>carried over</u>: $9 + 8 + 2 + 1 = \underline{20}$.
   So put '0' at the bottom and carry over the '2'.

4) Do the same for the <u>last column</u>: $2 + 4 + 2 = \underline{8}$.

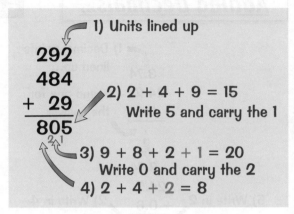

1) Units lined up

2) $2 + 4 + 9 = 15$
   Write 5 and carry the 1

3) $9 + 8 + 2 + 1 = 20$
   Write 0 and carry the 2

4) $2 + 4 + 2 = 8$

So $292 + 484 + 29 = \underline{805}$.

Subtracting

E.g. Work out 693 – 665

1) Line up the <u>units columns</u> of each number.

2) Going <u>right to left</u>, take the <u>bottom</u> number away from the <u>top</u> number.

   Here the top number (3) is <u>smaller</u> than the bottom number (5), so <u>borrow 10</u> from the next column along. The '9' in the tens column becomes '8'.

3) You now have $3 + 10 = \underline{13\ units}$, so you can do the subtraction $13 - 5 = \underline{8}$. Write the 8 at the <u>bottom</u>.

4) Subtracting the numbers in the <u>next column along</u> gives $8 - 6 = \underline{2}$, so write 2 at the <u>bottom</u>.

5) In the <u>last column</u>, $6 - 6 = \underline{0}$.

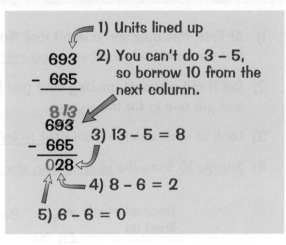

1) Units lined up

2) You can't do $3 - 5$, so borrow 10 from the next column.

3) $13 - 5 = 8$

4) $8 - 6 = 2$

5) $6 - 6 = 0$

So $693 - 665 = \underline{28}$.

Who needs a calculator when you have a pen and paper...

Test your skills of pen-and-paper maths with these teasers:
1) Work out: a) $56 + 738 + 12$, b) $459 - 273$.
2) When Ric was 10 he was 142 cm tall. Since then he has grown 29 cm.
   a) How tall is he now? b) How much taller must he be to be 190 cm tall?

Don't forget to include the units in your answers.

Adding and Subtracting Decimals

The <u>methods</u> for adding and subtracting <u>decimals</u> are <u>just the same</u> as the ones on the last page, but always make sure you <u>LINE UP THE DECIMAL POINTS</u>.

Adding Decimals...

E.g. Work out 3.74 + 24.2 + 0.6

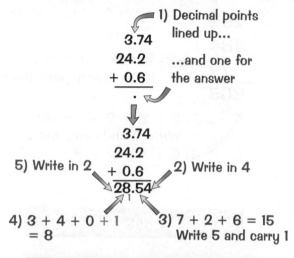

1) Decimal points lined up...

```
  3.74
 24.2
+ 0.6
```

...and one for the answer

```
  3.74
 24.2
+ 0.6
 28.54
```

5) Write in 2   2) Write in 4

4) 3 + 4 + 0 + 1 = 8   3) 7 + 2 + 6 = 15
                              Write 5 and carry 1

So 3.74 + 24.2 + 0.6 = <u>28.54</u>

1) <u>LINE UP THE DECIMAL POINTS</u> of each number, making sure all the other columns <u>line up</u>. Put a decimal point in the space for the <u>answer</u> too.

2) Add up the columns from <u>right to left</u>. The first column only has a 4 in it, so write <u>4</u> at the <u>bottom</u> of the column.

3) Add up the numbers in the <u>next column along</u>: 7 + 2 + 6 = <u>15</u>. Write the '5' at the <u>bottom</u> and <u>carry over</u> the '1' to the next column along.

4) Add up the <u>next column</u>, including anything <u>carried over</u>: 3 + 4 + 0 + 1 = <u>8</u>.

5) The <u>last column</u> just has a <u>2</u>, so write this in.

...and Subtracting Decimals

E.g. Bob has £8, but spends 26p on bubble-gum. How much is left?

1) At first, this question doesn't look like it has any <u>decimals</u> in it. But we need both numbers in <u>pounds</u> — so it becomes <u>£8.00 – £0.26</u>.

2) Set it out as usual, making sure you <u>LINE UP THE DECIMAL POINTS</u> and put one in for the <u>answer</u>.

3) Look at each column from <u>right to left</u>, taking away the <u>bottom number from the top</u>.

4) <u>Borrow 10</u> from the <u>next column along</u> if you need to, as before:

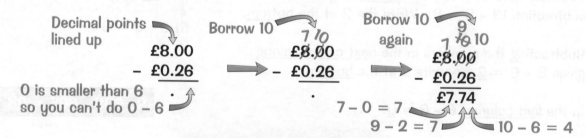

Decimal points lined up

```
  £8.00
– £0.26
```

0 is smaller than 6 so you can't do 0 – 6

Borrow 10

```
   7 10
  £8.00
– £0.26
```

Borrow 10 again

```
    9
   7 10 10
  £8.00
– £0.26
  £7.74
```

7 – 0 = 7
9 – 2 = 7   10 – 6 = 4

So £8.00 – £0.26 = <u>£7.74</u>.

Don't get short-changed — learn how to count your money...

In real life, you'll come across decimals most when dealing with money. Have a go at this:

1) I want to buy a packet of sweets for 54p and a magazine for £2.30.
   a) How much will I have to pay in total?   b) How much change will I have from a £5 note?

Multiplying by 10, 100, etc

You really should know the stuff on this page because:
a) it's <u>really useful</u>, and   b) they're likely to <u>test you on it</u> in the exam.

1) <u>To Multiply</u> Any Number by 10

Move the Decimal Point <u>ONE</u> place
<u>RIGHT</u> (⤳) and fill any gaps with <u>ZEROS</u>.

EXAMPLES:

23.6×10
$= 236$

345×10
$= 3450$

The gap's been filled with a zero.

2) <u>To Multiply</u> Any Number by <u>100</u>

Move the Decimal Point <u>TWO</u> places
<u>RIGHT</u> (⤳) and fill any gaps with <u>ZEROS</u>.

EXAMPLES:

34×100
$= 3400$

2.543×100
$= 254.3$

Gaps filled with zeros.

3) <u>To Multiply</u> by <u>1000 or 10 000</u>

Move the Decimal Point so many places
<u>RIGHT</u> (⤳) and fill any gaps with <u>ZEROS</u>.

EXAMPLES:

341×1000
$= 341000$

$2.3542 \times 10\,000$
$= 23542$

Gaps filled with zeros.

> You always <u>move</u> the <u>DECIMAL POINT</u> this much:
> <u>1 place for 10</u>,   <u>2 places for 100</u>,
> <u>3 places for 1000</u>,   <u>4 places for 10 000</u>   etc.

4) <u>To Multiply</u> by Numbers like 20, 300, 8000, etc.

<u>MULTIPLY</u> by <u>2</u> or <u>3</u> or <u>8</u> etc. <u>FIRST</u>, then move the
Decimal Point so many places <u>RIGHT</u> (⤳).

<u>EXAMPLE:</u> Find 234×2000.
1) <u>First multiply by 2</u>: $234 \times 2 = 468$
2) Then <u>move the DP 3 places right</u>: $468 \times 1000 = 468000$

The gaps have been filled with zeros.

<u>Go forth and multiply...</u>

<u>Four important methods</u> to learn here. For a bit of a workout, try these:
1) Work out   a) 345×10 b) 12.3×100 c) 9.65×1000 d) 60×3000

Dividing by 10, 100, etc

This is <u>useful</u> stuff too. So <u>make sure you know it</u> — that's all.

1) <u>To Divide Any Number by 10</u>

Move the Decimal Point <u>ONE</u> place <u>LEFT</u> (⌣) and if it's needed, <u>REMOVE ZEROS</u> after the decimal point.

<u>EXAMPLES:</u>

$23.6 \div 10$
$= \underline{2.36}$

$340 \div 10$
$= 34.0$
$= \underline{34}$

The zero after the decimal point has been removed.

2) <u>To Divide Any Number by 100</u>

Move the Decimal Point <u>TWO</u> places <u>LEFT</u> (⌣) and <u>REMOVE ZEROS</u> after the decimal point.

<u>EXAMPLES:</u>

$296.5 \div 100$
$= \underline{2.965}$

$340 \div 100$
$= 3.40$
$= \underline{3.4}$

Zero removed.

3) <u>To Divide by 1000 or 10 000</u>

Move the Decimal Point so many places <u>LEFT</u> (⌣) and <u>REMOVE ZEROS</u> after the decimal point.

You always <u>move</u> the <u>DECIMAL POINT</u> this much:
<u>1 place for 10</u>,   <u>2 places for 100</u>,
<u>3 places for 1000</u>,   <u>4 places for 10 000</u>   etc.

<u>EXAMPLES:</u>

$23500 \div 10\ 000$
$= 2.3500$
$= \underline{2.35}$ ← Zeros removed.

$341 \div 1000$
$= \underline{0.341}$

Fill in any gaps with zeros if you need to.

4) <u>To Divide by Numbers like 40, 300, 7000, etc.</u>

<u>DIVIDE</u> by <u>4</u> or <u>3</u> or <u>7</u> etc. <u>FIRST</u>, then move the Decimal Point so many places <u>LEFT</u> (⌣).

<u>EXAMPLE:</u> Find $960 \div 300$.
1) <u>First divide by 3</u>: $960 \div 3 = 320$
2) Then <u>move the DP 2 places left</u>: $320 \div 100 = 3.20$
3) You <u>don't need</u> the last zero after the decimal point, so the answer is <u>3.2</u>.

<u>Give this page your undivided attention...</u>

Knowing how to divide by <u>10, 100, 1000, etc.</u> will be very handy, so make sure you <u>learn this page</u>.
1) Work out   a) $2.45 \div 10$ b) $654.2 \div 100$ c) $3.08 \div 1000$ d) $32 \div 20$

Multiplying Without a Calculator

You need to be able to multiply numbers together <u>without a calculator</u> — for your <u>non-calculator exam</u>. There are <u>loads</u> of ways to do it, but these two are pretty good.

> E.g. Work out 46 × 27

The Grid Method

1) <u>Split up</u> each number into its <u>units</u> and <u>tens</u> (and <u>hundreds</u> and <u>thousands</u> if it has them). Look back at page 5 for how to do this.

> 46 = 40 + 6
> 27 = 20 + 7

2) Draw a <u>grid</u>, and <u>split it up</u> into how many 'bits' you've got. There are <u>4 bits</u> here (40, 6, 20 and 7).

	40	6
20		
7		

3) Write the 'bits' on the <u>outside</u> of the grid, like this:

4) <u>Multiply together</u> the 'bits' on the edge of each square (the stuff on page 9 will help). Write <u>each answer</u> in the middle of <u>each square</u>.

	40	6
20	40 × 20 = <u>800</u>	6 × 20 = <u>120</u>
7	40 × 7 = <u>280</u>	6 × 7 = <u>42</u>

5) <u>Add up</u> all the numbers inside the squares (see p. 7).

```
 800
 120
 280
 +42
-----
1242
  1
```

6) The <u>total</u> is your <u>final answer</u>.

> It helps if you know your <u>times tables</u>.

> So: 46 × 27 = <u>1242</u>

The 'Old' Way — how old people would have learnt it at school.

I won't go into detail with this — the grid method's a <u>lot easier</u> to learn.
But if you <u>know</u> how to do it this way then feel free to <u>use it</u>.

As you can see, the answer is <u>the same</u> either way.

```
    46
 ×  27
------
   322  —— This is 7 × 46
   920  —— This is 20 × 46
------
  1242  —— This is 322 + 920
```

> 46 × 27 = <u>1242</u>

Dividing Without a Calculator

OK, time for <u>dividing</u> now. Don't worry — here's a <u>tried-and-tested method</u> you can learn...

The 'Short Division' Method

EXAMPLE: "What is 714 ÷ 21?"

1) Set out the division as shown, with the <u>first</u> number inside the box, and the <u>second</u> number on the <u>outside</u>.

$21 \overline{)714}$

This is where the answer will go.

2) The first number in the box is <u>7</u>, so we say: "<u>How many times will 21 go into 7?</u>" The answer is <u>0</u> (because 21 is <u>bigger</u> than 7). So write a <u>0</u> over the 7 <u>above the box</u>.

$21 \overline{)7\,1\,4}^{\,0}$

21 into 7 doesn't go.

3) 21 didn't go into 7, so we try the <u>first two</u> numbers together — <u>71</u>. Count <u>how many lots of 21</u> will fit into <u>71</u> (keep adding lots of 21 until you get there).

21 + 21 = 42
42 + 21 = 63
63 + 21 = 84 — too big
So 21 + 21 + 21 = 21 × 3 = 63

4) 21 will go into 71 <u>3 times</u> (21 × 3 = 63) with <u>8 left over</u> (71 – 63 = 8). So write the <u>3 above the box</u> and <u>carry the 8</u> (called a <u>remainder</u>) over to the <u>next number</u> as shown.

$21 \overline{)7\,1\,{}^8 4}^{\,0\,3}$

Carry the 8.

21 into 71 goes 3 times, remainder 8.

5) Look at the <u>last number</u>, including the 8 carried over — this gives <u>84</u>. Count <u>how many lots of 21</u> will fit into <u>84</u>. You should find that it fits <u>exactly 4 times</u> with <u>no remainder</u>, so write the <u>4 above the box</u> as shown.

$21 \overline{)7\,1\,{}^8 4}^{\,0\,3\,4}$

21 into 84 goes 4 times exactly.

6) The number <u>on top</u> of the box is your <u>final answer</u>. (You can ignore the zero at the start.)

So 714 ÷ 21 = <u>34</u>.

<u>Sums without calculators — less painful than standing on a plug barefoot...</u>

Lots to take in there — it's really important that you learn the <u>methods</u> on these <u>two pages</u> though. Unless you know a different way that <u>always works</u> — in which case it's fine to use that. Read the last two pages again if you're still a bit unsure. Then try all of these <u>without</u> a calculator:

1) 28 × 12
2) 56 × 11
3) 104 × 8
4) 321 × 56
5) 242 ÷ 2
6) 84 ÷ 7
7) 96 ÷ 8
8) 275 ÷ 11

Special Number Sequences

You need to know all the types of number sequences on the next two pages.
They're all <u>special</u> in their very own way. Bless.

EVEN <u>Numbers all Divide by 2</u>

| 2 | 4 | 6 | 8 | 10 | 12 | 14 | 16 | 18 | 20... |

1) All <u>EVEN</u> numbers <u>END</u> in <u>0, 2, 4, 6 or 8</u>, e.g. 200, 342, 576, 94.

2) So any number that ends in one of these is <u>EVEN</u>, and can be <u>DIVIDED BY 2</u>.

ODD <u>Numbers Don't Divide by 2</u>

| 1 | 3 | 5 | 7 | 9 | 11 | 13 | 15 | 17 | 19 | 21 ... |

Everyone thought 3
was a little odd.

1) All <u>ODD</u> numbers <u>END</u> in <u>1, 3, 5, 7 or 9</u>, e.g. 301, 95, 807, 43.

2) So any number that ends in one of these is <u>ODD</u>, and <u>CAN'T</u> be divided by 2.

SQUARE <u>Numbers:</u>

1) They're called <u>SQUARE NUMBERS</u> because they're like the <u>areas</u> of this pattern of <u>squares</u>:

$1 \times 1 = 1$

$2 \times 2 = 4$

$3 \times 3 = 9$

$4 \times 4 = 16$

See page 29 for
more on areas.

(1×1) (2×2) (3×3) (4×4) (5×5) (6×6) (7×7) (8×8) (9×9) (10×10) (11×11) (12×12) (13×13) (14×14) (15×15)

| 1 | 4 | 9 | 16 | 25 | 36 | 49 | 64 | 81 | 100 | 121 | 144 | 169 | 196 | 225... |

3 5 7 9 11 13 15 17 19 21 23 25 27 29

2) Note that the <u>DIFFERENCES</u> between the <u>square numbers</u> are all the <u>ODD</u> numbers.

CUBE <u>Numbers:</u>

They're called <u>CUBE NUMBERS</u>
because they're like the <u>volumes</u> of
this pattern of <u>cubes</u>.

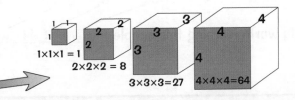

$1 \times 1 \times 1 = 1$

$2 \times 2 \times 2 = 8$

$3 \times 3 \times 3 = 27$

$4 \times 4 \times 4 = 64$

See page 31 for
more on volumes.

(1×1×1) (2×2×2) (3×3×3) (4×4×4) (5×5×5) (6×6×6) (7×7×7) (8×8×8) (9×9×9) (10×10×10)...

| 1 | 8 | 27 | 64 | 125 | 216 | 343 | 512 | 729 | 1000... |

Special Number Sequences

These next few sequences are a bit different from the others, but just as special.

POWERS:

1) Powers are 'numbers multiplied by themselves so many times'.

2) For example: 'Two to the power three' = 2^3 = $2 \times 2 \times 2 = 8$

The First Few POWERS OF 2:

| 2 | 4 | 8 | 16 | 32... |

$2^1=2$ $2^2=4$ $2^3=8$ $2^4=16$ etc...

To get the next number in the sequence, just times the last one by 2.

The First Few POWERS OF 10:

| 10 | 100 | 1000 | 10 000 | 100 000... |

$10^1=10$ $10^2=100$ $10^3=1000$ etc...

To get the next number in the sequence, just add an extra zero to the end of the last one.

TRIANGLE Numbers:

1) To remember the triangle numbers you have to picture in your mind this pattern of triangles, where each new row has one more blob than the previous row:

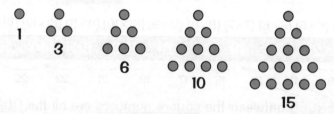

| 1 | 3 | 6 | 10 | 15 | 21 | 28 | 36 | 45 | 55 | ... |

2 3 4 5 6 7 8 9 10 11

2) It's definitely worth learning this simple pattern of differences between each of the numbers.

What do you do if your cube numbers are sad? Tell them they're special...

1) Cover up the last 2 pages and then write down the first 10 numbers in all seven sequences.

2) From this list of numbers: 23, 45, 56, 81, 25, 97, 134, 156, 125, 36, 64
write down: a) all the even numbers b) all the odd numbers c) all the square numbers
d) all the cube numbers e) all the powers of 2 f) all the triangle numbers.

Multiples, Factors and Primes

Hmm, the words above look <u>important</u>. Panic not — help is on its way...

Multiples

The __MULTIPLES__ of a number are just its __TIMES TABLE__.

E.g: The <u>multiples of 4</u> are: 4 8 12 16 20 24 28 32 36 ...
　　　The <u>multiples of 9</u> are: 9 18 27 36 45 54 63 72 ...

Factors

The __FACTORS__ of a number are all the numbers that <u>DIVIDE INTO IT</u>.

E.g. <u>8</u> goes <u>exactly</u> into <u>32</u>, so we say that 8 is a <u>factor</u> of 32.

You might be asked to find __ALL__ the factors of a number — <u>here's how to do it:</u>

__EXAMPLE:__ Find __ALL__ the factors of 24.

1) Start off with 1 × the number itself: 1 × 24 = 24.

2) Then try 2 × something to make 24.
   2 × 12 = 24, so this is the next row.

3) Now try 3 × something, and so on, listing the pairs in rows.

4) Try each one in turn and put a dash if it doesn't divide exactly.

5) Eventually, when you get a number <u>repeated</u>, you <u>stop</u>.

Increasing by 1 each time

1×24
2×12
3×8
4×6
$5 \times -$
6×4

So the __FACTORS OF 24__ are <u>1, 2, 3, 4, 6, 8, 12, 24</u>

PRIME Numbers Don't Divide by Anything

1) <u>Prime Numbers</u> are all the numbers that <u>DON'T</u> come up in <u>Times Tables</u> (other than <u>their own</u>):

2 3 5 7 11 13 17 19 23 29 31 37 ...

2) The <u>only way</u> to get __ANY PRIME NUMBER__ is: 1 × ITSELF

E.g: The <u>only</u> numbers that multiply to give 7 are:　1 × 7
　　　The <u>only</u> numbers that multiply to give 31 are:　1 × 31

Two is the oddest prime of all — it's the only one that's even...

Learn <u>all three sections</u> on this page, then <u>cover the stuff above</u> and have a go at these:
1) List the first 10 multiples of 6, and the first 10 multiples of 7.
2) List <u>all</u> the factors of 36.
3) Write down the first 10 prime numbers (without looking).

Fractions, Decimals and Percentages

Fractions, decimals and percentages are <u>three different ways</u> of showing a <u>proportion</u> (or part) of something. Read on to learn how to <u>switch between them</u>.

Fractions You Should Know

This table shows the proportions you should <u>know straight off</u>, without having to work them out:

Fraction	Decimal	Percentage
$\frac{1}{2}$	0.5	50%
$\frac{1}{4}$	0.25	25%
$\frac{3}{4}$	0.75	75%
$\frac{1}{3}$	0.33333... or 0.$\dot{3}$	$33\frac{1}{3}$%
$\frac{1}{10}$	0.1	10%
$\frac{2}{10}$	0.2	20%
$\frac{1}{5}$	0.2	20%

This is called a <u>recurring decimal</u> — the 3 keeps repeating itself <u>forever</u>.

How to Switch Between Them

For proportions <u>not</u> in the table above, use these <u>flowcharts</u> to help <u>switch</u> between the three types:

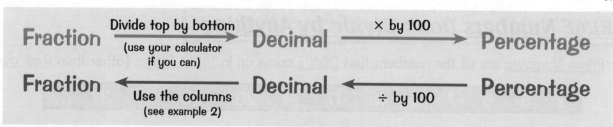

Fraction —Divide top by bottom (use your calculator if you can)→ Decimal —× by 100→ Percentage

Fraction ←Use the columns (see example 2)— Decimal ←÷ by 100— Percentage

<u>EXAMPLE 1</u>: $\frac{2}{5}$ is: $2 \div 5 = \underline{0.4}$ as a <u>decimal</u>, and $0.4 \times 100 = \underline{40\%}$ as a <u>percentage</u>.

<u>EXAMPLE 2</u>: <u>30%</u> is: $30 \div 100 = \underline{0.3}$ as a <u>decimal</u>.

The 3 is in the <u>tenths column</u>, so it's '<u>three tenths</u>' or $\frac{3}{10}$ as a <u>fraction</u>.

If the fraction's not in its <u>simplest form</u> you need to <u>cancel down</u> — see next page.

Oh, what's recurrin'?...

Knowing all of the <u>top table</u> and the <u>flowchart</u> will help you loads in the exam.

1) Turn the following decimals into fractions and percentages: a) 0.7   b) 0.01   c) 0.6

Fractions

This page tells you how to deal with fractions <u>without your calculator</u>.
Make sure that you can do <u>everything</u> explained here. Every last bit.

Equivalent Fractions

$\frac{1}{4}$ ...is equivalent to... $\frac{4}{16}$

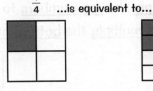

1) <u>Equivalent</u> fractions are <u>equal in size</u>...
2) ...but the <u>numbers</u> on the top and bottom are <u>different</u>.
3) To get from one fraction to an equivalent one —
   <u>MULTIPLY top and bottom</u> by the <u>SAME NUMBER</u>:

$$\frac{1}{2} \xrightarrow{\times 3} = \xrightarrow{\times 3} \frac{3}{6} \qquad \frac{3}{4} \xrightarrow{\times 5} = \xrightarrow{\times 5} \frac{15}{20} \qquad \frac{1}{5} \xrightarrow{\times 100} = \xrightarrow{\times 100} \frac{100}{500}$$

Cancelling Down

1) You sometimes need to <u>simplify</u> a fraction by '<u>cancelling down</u>'.
2) This means <u>DIVIDING top and bottom</u> by the <u>SAME NUMBER</u>.
3) To get the fraction <u>as simple as possible</u>,
   you might have to do this <u>more than once</u>:

$$\frac{3}{15} \xrightarrow{\div 3} = \xrightarrow{\div 3} \frac{1}{5}$$

$$\frac{20}{40} \xrightarrow{\div 10} = \xrightarrow{\div 10} \frac{2}{4} \xrightarrow{\div 2} = \xrightarrow{\div 2} \frac{1}{2}$$

Ordering Fractions — Put Them Over the Same Number

E.g. Which is <u>bigger</u>, $\frac{2}{3}$ or $\frac{3}{4}$?

1) Look at the <u>bottom numbers</u> ('denominators') of the fractions: <u>3</u> and <u>4</u>.
2) Think of a number they will <u>both go into</u> — try <u>12</u>.
3) <u>Change</u> each fraction (make <u>equivalent</u> fractions) so the <u>bottom number is 12</u>.

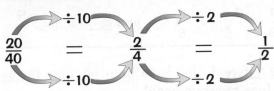

$$\frac{2}{3} \xrightarrow{\times 4} = \frac{8}{12} \qquad \frac{3}{4} \xrightarrow{\times 3} = \frac{9}{12}$$

4) Now check which is biggest by looking at their <u>top numbers</u> ('numerators').
5) 9 is <u>bigger</u> than 8, so $\frac{3}{4}$ is bigger than $\frac{2}{3}$.

LIGHTS... CAMERA... FRACTION...

Have a go at <u>cancelling down</u> and <u>ordering the fractions</u> below — and no cheating with a calculator.

1) Cancel these down as far as possible: a) $\frac{30}{36}$ b) $\frac{18}{27}$ 2) Which is bigger, $\frac{3}{5}$ or $\frac{2}{3}$?

Fractions

Here are some <u>more ways</u> to cope with fractions <u>without your calculator</u>. Aren't I kind.

Multiplying

1) <u>Multiply</u> the <u>top numbers</u> to make the new top number (<u>numerator</u>)...

2) ...and <u>multiply</u> the <u>bottom numbers</u> to make the new bottom number (<u>denominator</u>).

$$\text{E.g. } \frac{3}{5} \times \frac{4}{7} = \frac{3 \times 4}{5 \times 7} = \frac{12}{35}$$

Dividing

1) Turn the 2nd fraction <u>UPSIDE DOWN</u>...

2) ...and then <u>multiply</u>, as shown above.

2nd fraction is now upside down.

$$\text{E.g. } \frac{3}{4} \div \frac{1}{3} = \frac{3}{4} \times \frac{3}{1} = \frac{3 \times 3}{4 \times 1} = \frac{9}{4}$$

Adding and Subtracting

1) If the <u>bottom numbers</u> are the <u>same</u>, add or subtract <u>TOP NUMBERS ONLY</u>, leaving the bottom number <u>as it is</u>.

$$\text{E.g. } \underline{\text{adding}}: \frac{2}{6} + \frac{1}{6} = \frac{2+1}{6} = \frac{3}{6} \qquad \text{and } \underline{\text{subtracting}}: \frac{5}{7} - \frac{3}{7} = \frac{5-3}{7} = \frac{2}{7}$$

2) If the bottom numbers are <u>different</u>, you have to <u>make them the same</u> using <u>equivalent fractions</u> (see previous page).

$$\text{E.g. to do } \frac{1}{2} + \frac{1}{4}, \text{ turn the } \frac{1}{2} \text{ into } \frac{2}{4} \text{ and then } \underline{\text{add as usual}}: \frac{2}{4} + \frac{1}{4} = \frac{2+1}{4} = \frac{3}{4}$$

Finding a Fraction of Something — Just Multiply then Divide

1) <u>Multiply</u> the 'something' by the <u>TOP</u> of the fraction...

2) ...then <u>divide</u> it by the <u>BOTTOM</u>.

$$\text{E.g. } \frac{9}{20} \text{ of } £360 = £360 \times 9 \div 20 = \underline{£162}$$

In other words, £162 is $\frac{9}{20}$ of £360.

'The Denominator' — maths robot from the future...

Now you've learnt these <u>useful tips</u>, it's time to have a go at these below — <u>without</u> a calculator.

1) a) $\frac{3}{4} \times \frac{5}{6}$ b) $\frac{4}{5} \div \frac{7}{8}$ c) $\frac{3}{8} + \frac{1}{8}$ d) $\frac{4}{5} - \frac{2}{5}$ e) $\frac{3}{10} + \frac{2}{5}$

Ratios

A ratio is just another way of showing a <u>proportion</u> of something (like fractions, decimals and %).
E.g. splitting something in the <u>ratio 1:2</u> means that the <u>second</u> part is <u>twice as big</u> as the <u>first</u> part.
Most exam questions on <u>ratios</u> can be done using the <u>GOLDEN RULE</u>...

DIVIDE FOR ONE, THEN TIMES FOR ALL

Example: "5 pints of milk cost £1.30. How much will 3 pints cost?"

1) The <u>GOLDEN RULE</u> says: **DIVIDE FOR ONE, THEN TIMES FOR ALL**

2) So first <u>divide the price by 5</u> to find how much it costs <u>FOR ONE PINT</u>:

$$£1.30 ÷ 5 = 0.26 = \underline{26p} \text{ (for 1 pint)}$$

3) Then <u>times by 3</u> to find how much it costs <u>FOR 3 PINTS</u>:

$$\underline{26p} × 3 = \underline{78p} \text{ (for 3 pints)}$$

My favourite cereal is muesli.

Splitting Into Ratios

Sometimes you need to <u>SPLIT AN AMOUNT</u> into a certain <u>RATIO</u>.

EXAMPLE: "£5000 is to be divided in the ratio 1:4. Find the two amounts."

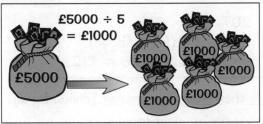
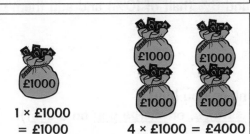

1) £5000 is split into <u>5 equal parts</u> (because 1 + 4 = <u>5</u>).

$$£5000 ÷ 5 \text{ parts} = \underline{£1000 \text{ per part}}$$

2) The <u>first</u> person in the ratio 1:4 gets <u>1 part</u>...

$$1 × £1000 = \underline{£1000}$$

3) ...and the <u>second</u> person gets <u>4 parts</u>.

$$4 × £1000 = \underline{£4000}$$

4) So the two amounts are <u>£1000:£4000</u>.

Simplifying Ratios

<u>Simplifying ratios</u> is the same as <u>cancelling down fractions</u> (see page 17).
E.g. for the ratio <u>15:18</u>, 3 will go into both numbers so <u>divide them by 3</u> — that gives <u>5:6</u>.

Remember — "divide for one, then times for all"...

It's a simple rule — the trick is knowing <u>when to use it</u>. Learning the <u>examples above</u> will help.
1) If seven pencils cost 70p, how much will 4 pencils cost? 2) Divide £1200 in the ratio 5:7.

Percentages

Percentages crop up all the time in real life — and they're bound to be in the exam.
There are two important details to remember:

> 1) 'Per cent' (%) means 'out of 100',
> e.g. 20% means '20 out of 100' = $\dfrac{20}{100}$
>
> 2) 'OF' means 'times' ('×')
> e.g. 20% of £60 = $\dfrac{20}{100} \times £60$

'Percentage Of' Questions

E.g. "Find 20% of £60."

1) This is the method to use if you have a calculator:

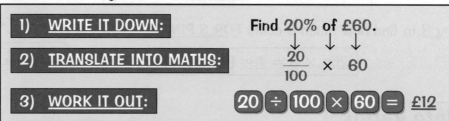

> 1) **WRITE IT DOWN:** Find 20% of £60.
> 2) **TRANSLATE INTO MATHS:** $\dfrac{20}{100} \times 60$
> 3) **WORK IT OUT:** 20 ÷ 100 × 60 = £12

2) If you don't have a calculator, you can do it this way:

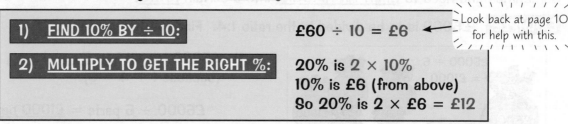

> 1) **FIND 10% BY ÷ 10:** £60 ÷ 10 = £6   ← Look back at page 10 for help with this.
> 2) **MULTIPLY TO GET THE RIGHT %:**
> 20% is 2 × 10%
> 10% is £6 (from above)
> So 20% is 2 × £6 = £12

This way also works for things like 5% — just find 10% then halve the answer (divide by 2).

For something like 35% — find 30% (3 lots of 10%) and 5% (half of 10%) and add them up.

% Discount and % Interest

1) You might see questions about discounts (money off things you buy)
   or interest (money that the bank can give you on your savings, or charge you on a debt).

2) There's an extra bit to these sorts of questions.

3) First find the 'percentage of'. Then ADD IT ON (for interest or increase questions)
   or TAKE IT AWAY (for discount or decrease questions).

> **EXAMPLE:** In the sale, a jacket which usually costs £60 has a discount of 20%.
> Find the reduced price of the jacket.

ANSWER:

1) First find 20% of £60. We know from the last example that it's £12.

2) This £12 is the DISCOUNT so we take it away from the original price to get the final answer:
   £60 − £12 = £48, so the reduced price is £48.

Revision Test for Section One

1) Write this number out <u>in words</u>: 1 306 515 *one million, three hundred and six thousand, five hundred and fifteen.*

2) Put these numbers in <u>order of size</u>, smallest to biggest:
   a) ~~23~~   6534   ~~123~~   ~~2200~~   ~~2~~   ~~132~~   789   ~~45~~ *2, 23, 45, 123, 132, 2200, 6534*
   b) ~~0.01~~   ~~0.12~~   ~~0.003~~   ~~0.05~~   ~~0.6~~   ~~0.0021~~
   0.0021, 0.003, 0.01, 0.05, 0.12, 0.6

<u>DON'T</u> use your calculator for questions 3-7

3) <u>Work out</u>: a) 756 + 328 + 61   b) 456 – 291   c) 8.63 + 2.1 + 0.4
   1135

4) Alvin wants to buy a pet fish (costing <u>£6.45</u>) and some fish food (costing <u>£1.34</u>).
   a) How much will this cost <u>in total</u>?   b) How much <u>change</u> will he have from £10.00?
   =£7.79   *= £2.21*

5) Jan needs to buy <u>100</u> large envelopes at <u>£1.20</u> each.
   How much money does she need?   *£120*   Hint: 1.20 × 100.

6) Chris bought <u>100</u> chocolate bars for <u>£32</u> to sell in the school tuck shop.
   How much should he sell each chocolate bar for to make his money back?   Hint: 32 ÷ 100.
   = 32p

7) <u>Work out</u>: a) 69 × 11   b) 145 ÷ 5

8) What are <u>square numbers</u>? Write down the <u>first five</u> of them.

9) Find <u>all the factors</u> of 30. *1, 30, 2, 15, 3, 10, 5, 6*

10) What is <u>60%</u> as: a) a <u>decimal</u>?   b) a <u>fraction</u>? *$\frac{3}{5}$*
                            = 0.6

11) Cancel down $\frac{25}{100}$ as far as possible so it's in its <u>simplest form</u>. *$= \frac{5}{20} = \frac{1}{4}$*

12) Which is <u>bigger</u>, $\frac{7}{8}$ or $\frac{3}{4}$? *$= \frac{7}{8}$*

13) Work out <u>without</u> a calculator: a) $\frac{2}{3} \times \frac{2}{5}$ b) $\frac{5}{6} \div \frac{8}{3}$ c) $\frac{5}{8} + \frac{2}{8}$ *$= \frac{7}{8}$*   d) $\frac{5}{7} - \frac{3}{7}$ *$= \frac{2}{7}$*
    $= \frac{4}{15}$ *$= \frac{15}{48}$*

14) Grandma Wolfe has <u>£800</u> to split between her two grandchildren in the <u>ratio 1:3</u>.
    How much does <u>each child</u> get? *£200 : £600*

15) Carl puts £300 in the bank. He makes <u>5% interest</u> on his money.
    a) What is <u>5% of £300</u>?   b) How much money does he have <u>in total</u>?

Symmetry

There are <u>TWO types</u> of symmetry, and guess what — you need to know about them <u>both</u>.

1) <u>Line Symmetry is...</u>

...where you draw a <u>MIRROR LINE</u> across a picture and <u>both sides will fold exactly together</u>.

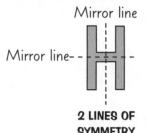
Mirror line

Mirror line

| 2 LINES OF SYMMETRY | 1 LINE OF SYMMETRY | 1 LINE OF SYMMETRY | 3 LINES OF SYMMETRY | NO LINES OF SYMMETRY | 1 LINE OF SYMMETRY |

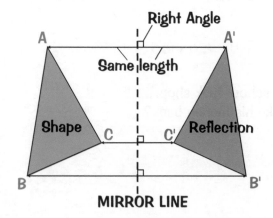

Right Angle

Same length

A   A'

Shape   C   C'   Reflection

B   B'

MIRROR LINE

<u>How to Draw a Reflection:</u>

1) <u>Label each corner</u> of the shape (e.g. A, B, C...)
2) From point A, <u>draw a line</u> at <u>right angles</u> to the mirror line.
3) <u>Carry on</u> the line to the <u>other side</u> of the mirror line.
4) Mark a point at <u>exactly the same distance</u> away from the mirror line as A. Call this A'.
5) <u>Repeat</u> for all the other points.
6) <u>Join up the points</u> (A', B' and C') to make the <u>reflection</u>.

2) <u>Rotational Symmetry is...</u>

...where you <u>turn</u> (rotate) a shape around into different positions that <u>all look exactly the same</u>.

1) The '<u>order</u>' means <u>how many</u> different positions <u>look the same</u>.
2) For '<u>order 1</u>', only <u>one position</u> is the same. It has <u>no rotational symmetry</u>.

This 'S' looks the same <u>2 ways</u> — turn the book around and see.

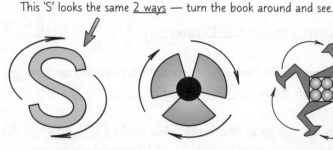
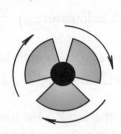

| Order 1 | Order 2 | Order 2 | Order 3 | Order 4 |

Symmetry and Tessellations

Tracing Paper Makes Things Easier

1) You can ask for tracing paper in the EXAM — here's how you can use it:

2) For LINE SYMMETRY:

- Trace half the shape and the mirror line.
- Flip the paper over and line up the mirror lines.
- If there's line symmetry, the tracing should match the other half of the shape.

3) For ROTATIONAL SYMMETRY:

- Trace round the shape.
- Spin the tracing paper round and count how many times it 'fits' onto the shape on the paper.
- This is the order of rotational symmetry.

Example Shape

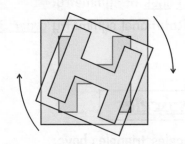

Tessellations

1) The name 'tessellation' means 'A TILING PATTERN WITH NO GAPS':

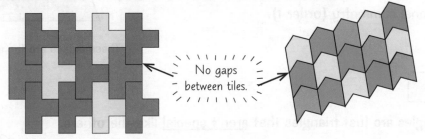

No gaps between tiles.

2) In the exam, you can be asked to tessellate shapes.

EXAMPLE: Baz has bought two types of tile to cover his kitchen floor. On the grid, show how the tiles will tessellate.

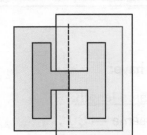

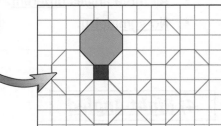

To do this, just make sure you only use the shapes given, and that they fit together exactly with no gaps or overlapping bits.

Ask for tracing paper if you need it — trace around the tiles and move them around to see where they fit.

Remember — your pattern shouldn't have any gaps.

Mirror mirror on the wall, who's the most symmetrical of all?

Make sure you know the two types of symmetry and what tessellations are. Then look at each letter below and say how many lines of symmetry it has, and what the order of rotational symmetry is.

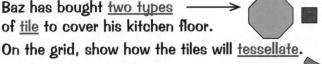

H   Z   T   N   E   X

2D Shapes

2D shapes are <u>flat shapes</u>. There are loads of <u>different types</u>, and they're special in <u>different ways</u> (just like your mates). Make sure you know all the ones on the next two pages.

Three-sided Shapes — Triangles

1) Equilateral

<u>Equilateral</u> triangles have:

- All <u>3 sides</u> the <u>same length</u>.
- All <u>3 angles</u> the same — <u>60°</u>.
- <u>3 lines</u> of symmetry.
- Rotational symmetry <u>order 3</u> (see p. 22).

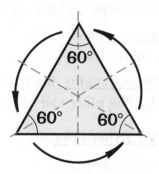

2) Isosceles

<u>Isosceles</u> triangles have:

- <u>2 sides</u> the same length.
- <u>2 angles</u> the same.
- <u>1 line</u> of symmetry.
- <u>No</u> rotational symmetry (order 1).

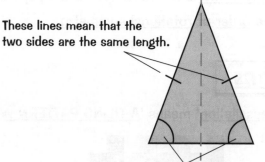

These lines mean that the two sides are the same length.

These angles are the same.

3) Scalene

<u>Scalene</u> triangles are just triangles that <u>aren't special</u> like the others.

- All three sides <u>different lengths</u>.
- All three angles <u>different</u>.
- <u>No symmetry</u>.

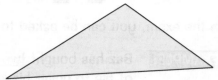

4) Right-Angled

1) <u>Right-angled</u> triangles have a <u>right-angle</u> (<u>90°</u>) somewhere.
2) They can also be <u>isosceles</u> or <u>scalene</u>.
3) Right-angled triangles have:

- 1 <u>right angle</u> (90°).
- <u>No lines</u> of <u>symmetry</u> (unless it's <u>isosceles</u> too).
- <u>No rotational symmetry</u> (order 1).

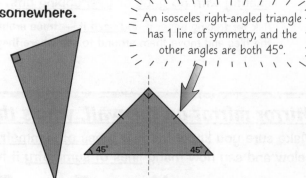

An isosceles right-angled triangle has 1 line of symmetry, and the other angles are both 45°.

45°   45°

2D Shapes

Four-sided Shapes — Quadrilaterals

1) SQUARE

 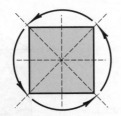

- <u>All sides</u> the <u>same length</u>.
- <u>All angles</u> the same (<u>90°</u>).
- <u>4 lines</u> of symmetry.
- Rotational symmetry <u>order 4</u>.

2) RECTANGLE

 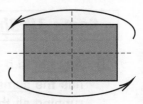

- <u>2 pairs of sides</u> the <u>same length</u>.
- <u>All angles</u> the same (<u>90°</u>).
- <u>2 lines</u> of symmetry.
- Rotational symmetry <u>order 2</u>.

3) RHOMBUS   (A square pushed over.)

These arrows mean <u>parallel sides</u> (see p.49).

 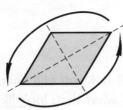

- <u>All sides</u> the <u>same length</u>.
- <u>2 pairs</u> of <u>parallel sides</u>.
- <u>2 lines</u> of symmetry.
- Rotational symmetry <u>order 2</u>.

4) PARALLELOGRAM   (A rectangle pushed over.)

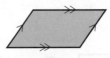 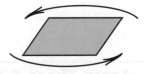

- <u>2 pairs of sides</u> the <u>same length</u>.
- <u>2 pairs</u> of <u>parallel sides</u>.
- <u>NO lines</u> of symmetry.
- Rotational symmetry <u>order 2</u>.

5) TRAPEZIUM

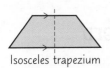 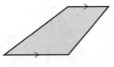

Isosceles trapezium

- <u>One pair</u> of parallel sides
- <u>Only</u> the <u>isosceles trapezium</u> has a <u>line</u> of symmetry.
- <u>None</u> have rotational symmetry.

6) KITE

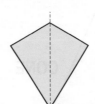

- <u>1 line</u> of symmetry.
- <u>No rotational symmetry</u>.

Rhombus facts: 4 sides, 2 lines of symmetry, Gemini, peanut allergy...

Learn <u>everything on these pages</u>. Then turn over and say all the details that you can remember. Then try again. It's as simple as that. Then you can play with the kite. Indoors though — it's new.

3D Shapes

I was going to make some pop-out <u>3D shapes</u> to put on this page, but I couldn't find the scissors and sticky tape. Sorry.

3D Shapes Are Solid Shapes

Some 3D Shapes Are Called <u>Prisms</u>:

1) A <u>prism</u> is a <u>3D shape</u> which has the <u>same sized shape</u> running all the way through it.

2) E.g. if you <u>slice up</u> a <u>cylinder</u> (like <u>slicing a cucumber</u>) the <u>end face</u> of each slice will be the same — <u>a circle</u>.

3) We say that prisms have a '<u>constant area of cross-section</u>'.

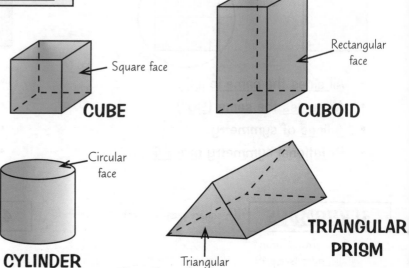

Square face
CUBE

Rectangular face
CUBOID

Circular face
CYLINDER

Triangular face
TRIANGULAR PRISM

Learn These 4 Too:

These <u>AREN'T PRISMS</u> but you still have to know their <u>names</u> and what they <u>look like</u>:

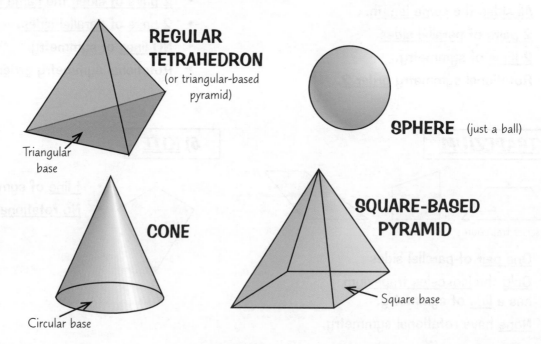

REGULAR TETRAHEDRON
(or triangular-based pyramid)

Triangular base

SPHERE (just a ball)

CONE

Circular base

SQUARE-BASED PYRAMID

Square base

Well done — you've moved on to solids...

Deep breath in... and out... then learn the <u>eight 3D shapes</u> on this page.
Then cover up the page and see if you can name all eight different types of solid object.

Regular Polygons

A <u>polygon</u> is a <u>many-sided shape</u>.   <u>Regular polygons</u> have some fancy features for you to learn.

A <u>REGULAR</u> polygon is one where <u>ALL THE SIDES AND ANGLES</u> are the <u>SAME</u>.

You Need to Know These <u>Regular Polygons:</u>

EQUILATERAL *TRIANGLE*

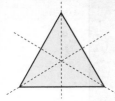

- <u>3 sides</u>
- <u>3 lines</u> of symmetry
- Rotational symmetry <u>order 3</u>

You should remember this from page 24.

SQUARE

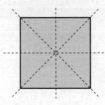

- <u>4 sides</u>
- <u>4 lines</u> of symmetry
- Rotational symmetry <u>order 4</u>

This was on page 25.

REGULAR *PENTAGON*

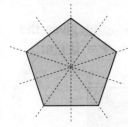

- <u>5 sides</u>
- <u>5 lines</u> of symmetry
- Rotational symmetry <u>order 5</u>

REGULAR *HEXAGON*

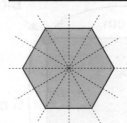

- <u>6 sides</u>
- <u>6 lines</u> of symmetry
- Rotational symmetry <u>order 6</u>

REGULAR *HEPTAGON*

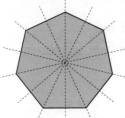

- <u>7 sides</u>
- <u>7 lines</u> of symmetry
- Rotational symmetry <u>order 7</u>

(A 50p piece is like a heptagon)

REGULAR *OCTAGON*

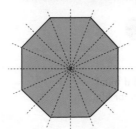

- <u>8 sides</u>
- <u>8 lines</u> of symmetry
- Rotational symmetry <u>order 8</u>

Remember — <u>any</u> 8-sided shape will be called an octagon, but a <u>regular</u> octagon must have <u>all sides and angles the same</u>.

EXCLUSIVE: Heptagon lottery winner says "I'm still just a regular guy"...

For regular polygons: number of <u>sides</u> = number of <u>lines of symmetry</u> = <u>order of rotational symmetry</u>.

1) What is a regular polygon?   2) Name the first six of them without looking at the page.

Perimeters

Perimeter is the distance <u>all the way around the outside of a shape</u>.
It helps if you can use the <u>big blob method</u> to work it out...

Perimeter is the Distance Around the Edge of a Shape

1) To find a <u>PERIMETER</u>, you <u>ADD UP THE LENGTHS OF ALL THE SIDES</u>.

2) To make sure you get <u>all the sides</u>, do this:

> 1) <u>PUT A BIG BLOB AT ONE CORNER</u> and then go around the shape.
>
> 2) <u>WRITE DOWN THE LENGTH OF EVERY SIDE</u> as you go along.
>
> 3) <u>DON'T FORGET SIDES THAT SEEM TO HAVE NO LENGTH GIVEN</u>
>   — <u>you must work them out first (see example)</u>.
>
> 4) Keep going until you get back to the <u>BIG BLOB</u>.

<u>EXAMPLE</u>: Find the perimeter of the shape below.

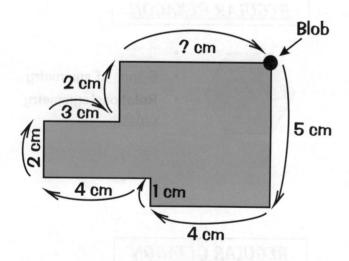

You must choose yourself a blob and it must
also choose you. It will then be yours for life.

1) Check you know <u>all the sides' lengths</u>.
   One is <u>missing</u> here, so <u>find this first</u>.

2) Adding up the <u>bottom lengths</u> gives the
   <u>width</u> of the shape: 4 + 4 = <u>8 cm</u>:

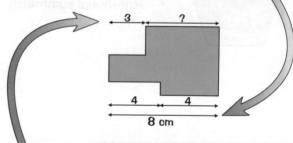

This must be the <u>same</u> across the <u>top</u>, so
the missing length must be 8 – 3 = <u>5 cm</u>.

3) So the perimeter must be:
   5+4+1+4+2+3+2+5 = <u>26 cm</u>.

RUN — DON'T WALK from... the BIG BLOB...

...no, don't do that really. You need to get friendly with your big blob,
and always use him for finding the perimeter of shapes.
He should always be willing to help — if not, just feed him a calculator
or two and he'll be happy in no time. He also quite likes cheese.

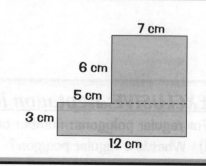

1) <u>Turn over and write down</u> what a perimeter is.

2) Find the perimeter of the shape shown here.

Section Two — Shapes and Area

Areas

First things first — below are <u>three formulas</u> to work out the <u>areas</u> of shapes.
You need to <u>learn these</u>. Unless you want to <u>wave goodbye</u> to loads of exam marks...

You must LEARN these Formulas:

1) RECTANGLE

Width

Length

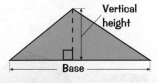

area   length   width

Area of <u>RECTANGLE</u> = length × width

<u>Example:</u>   Area = length × width
            Area = 12 m × 5 m
            Area = <u>60 m²</u>.

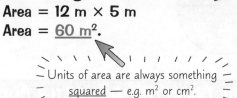

— Units of area are always something —
<u>squared</u> — e.g. m² or cm².

5 m

12 m

2) TRIANGLE

Vertical height

Base

$$A = \tfrac{1}{2} \times b \times h_v$$

base   vertical height

Area of <u>TRIANGLE</u> = ½ × base × vertical height

The <u>height</u> is always the <u>vertical height</u>, <u>not</u> the <u>sloping height</u>.

<u>Example:</u>   Area = ½ × base × height
            Area = ½ × 3 cm × 4 cm
            Area = <u>6 cm²</u>.

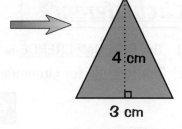

4 cm

3 cm

3) PARALLELOGRAM

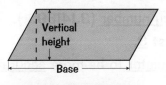

Vertical height

Base

$$A = b \times h_v$$

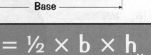

Area of <u>PARALLELOGRAM</u> = base × vertical height

<u>Example:</u>   Area = base × height
            Area = 5 cm × 3 cm
            Area = <u>15 cm²</u>.

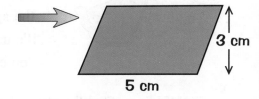

3 cm

5 cm

— Again, use the <u>vertical height</u>, —
not the sloping height.

Make this your best area of maths...

Did I mention that you need to <u>learn the formulas</u>? <u>Cover them up</u> on the page, and have a go at these:
1) What is the area of a rectangle with length 8 cm and width 5 cm?
2) A triangle has a 10 cm base and a vertical height of 4 cm. What is the area of the triangle?

Circles

There are quite a few things about <u>circles</u> you need to know.
It's probably best to have a snack before starting this page. All the talk of <u>pi</u> can make you hungry.

Diameter <u>and</u> Radius

1) The <u>DIAMETER</u> goes <u>right across</u> the circle, through the <u>centre</u> (middle).

2) The <u>RADIUS</u> only goes <u>halfway</u> across, from the <u>centre</u> (middle).

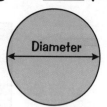

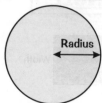

THE DIAMETER IS EXACTLY DOUBLE THE RADIUS

<u>EXAMPLES</u>: If the radius is 4 cm, the diameter is 4 cm × 2 = <u>8 cm</u>.

If the diameter is 24 m, the radius is 24 m ÷ 2 = <u>12 m</u>.

Circumference

1) The <u>CIRCUMFERENCE</u> is the <u>distance</u> round the <u>outside</u> of the circle.

2) The <u>formula</u> for circumference is:

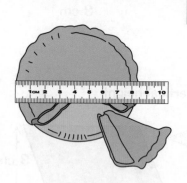

$$\text{Circumference} = \pi \times \text{Diameter}$$

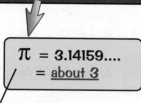

$\pi = 3.14159....$
$= \underline{\text{about } 3}$

The symbol π (called "<u>pi</u>") is just an <u>ordinary number</u> (3.14159...).
It's usually <u>rounded off</u> to <u>3.142</u> or even just <u>3</u>.
You can also use the π button on your <u>calculator</u> to be more <u>accurate</u>.

<u>EXAMPLE</u>: Find the <u>circumference</u> of a circle with <u>radius 5 cm</u>.

<u>ANSWER</u>: First find the <u>diameter</u>, which is <u>double the radius</u>: 5 × 2 = <u>10 cm</u>.
Then use the <u>formula</u>: Circumference = π × Diameter = 3.142 × 10 = <u>31.42 cm</u>.

<u>Common mistake — a slice of pie is not called a wedgie...</u>

Once again, learn it all, turn over and see what you can remember. If you can remember it all, reward yourself with a pie of your choice. Do I want a wedgie? Oh, well, if you're offering it's rude not to...

Volume

Learn the <u>formulas</u> on this page and you'll be able to find the <u>volumes</u> of loads of <u>3D shapes</u>.

1) Cuboid (rectangular block)

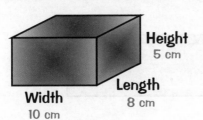

Height
5 cm

Width
10 cm

Length
8 cm

<u>Volume of Cuboid</u> = length × width × height

$$V = l \times w \times h$$

E.g. <u>Volume</u> = 8 × 10 × 5 = <u>400 cm³</u>.

Units of volume are always something <u>cubed</u> — e.g. m³ or cm³.

2) Prism

1) <u>A PRISM</u> is a solid (3D) shape which is the <u>same shape</u> all the way through — it has a <u>CONSTANT AREA OF CROSS-SECTION</u> (see page 26).

Triangular Prism

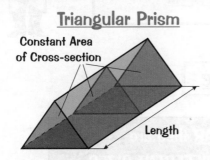

Constant Area of Cross-section

Length

Circular Prism (or Cylinder)

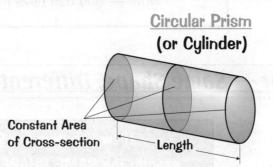

Constant Area of Cross-section

Length

2) The <u>formula</u> for the <u>volume of a prism</u> is:

$$\text{Volume of prism} = \text{Cross-sectional Area} \times \text{length}$$

$$V = A \times l$$

<u>EXAMPLE:</u> Find the volume of this <u>triangular prism</u>. ⟶

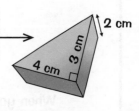

2 cm
3 cm
4 cm

<u>ANSWER:</u> First find the <u>area of the cross-section</u> using the formula for the <u>area of a triangle</u> (see p. 29).

Area = ½ × base × height = ½ × 4 × 3 = 6 cm².

Now use the formula for volume: **V** = A × l = 6 × 2 = <u>12 cm³</u>.

<u>Don't make it any more angry — it's already a cross-section...</u>

Once you've learnt the formulas, just put the right numbers in and the answer is yours.
All yours. Mwah-ha-ha-ha-haaaaaa.   1) Find the volume of this cuboid:
(Don't forget the units).

3 m
1.5 m
2 m

Congruence and Similarity

Shapes can be <u>congruent</u> or <u>similar</u>. And I bet you <u>really</u> want to know what that means. Well, lucky you — I've written a page all about it.

Congruent — Same Shape, Same Size

If two shapes are <u>CONGRUENT</u>, they are simply <u>THE SAME</u> — <u>the SAME SIZE</u> and the <u>SAME SHAPE</u>.

E.g. The shapes below are all <u>congruent</u>. They've just been drawn in <u>different positions</u>.

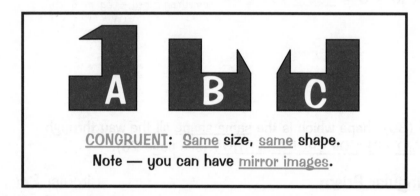

<u>CONGRUENT</u>: <u>Same</u> size, <u>same</u> shape.
Note — you can have <u>mirror images</u>.

There ain't room for the two of us in this town, pal.

Similar — Same Shape, Different Size

If two shapes are <u>SIMILAR</u> they are exactly the <u>SAME SHAPE</u> but <u>DIFFERENT SIZES</u>.

Two similar shapes can be seen as an '<u>enlargement</u>'... see page 52.

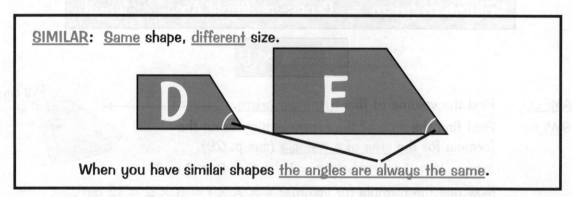

<u>SIMILAR</u>: <u>Same</u> shape, <u>different</u> size.

When you have similar shapes <u>the angles are always the same</u>.

Pizza and a frisbee — same shape and size but don't get them confused...

Know what congruent and similar mean —
it's important you don't get them mixed up.

1) a) Which of these four shapes are similar? i) ii) iii) iv)
   b) Which are congruent?

Section Two — Shapes and Area

Revision Test for Section Two

1) Sharon is making some birthday cards. She wants to fold each
card along a <u>line of symmetry</u>, so it folds exactly together.
Draw <u>all</u> the lines of symmetry for each of the card designs.
   a)    b) 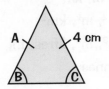   c)

2) Give the <u>order of rotational symmetry</u> for each of the designs above.

3) The shape on the right is an <u>isosceles</u> triangle.
   a) What is the <u>length</u> of side A?
   b) What's special about <u>angles B and C</u>?

4) What <u>4-sided shape</u> has all its sides the <u>same length</u> AND only <u>2 lines</u> of symmetry?

5) Sketch these four shapes, and say which are <u>prisms</u>:
   a) <u>Triangular Prism</u>   b) <u>Cone</u>   c) <u>Cylinder</u>   d) <u>Sphere</u>

6) Write down everything you know about <u>regular octagons</u>.

7) Alison wants to put a fence around the whole <u>perimeter</u> of her garden, shown below.
   a) Work out the <u>missing length</u> on the plan of the garden.
   b) How many <u>metres</u> of fencing should Alison buy?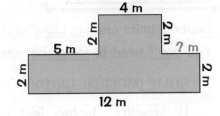

8) Clive is re-carpeting his lounge, which is <u>rectangular</u>.
   The room is <u>12 m long</u> and <u>7 m wide</u>.
   What <u>area</u> of carpet does he need?

9) Find the <u>area</u> of:
   a) a <u>triangle</u> with base <u>4 cm</u> and vertical height <u>9 cm</u>.
   b) a <u>parallelogram</u> with base <u>12 cm</u> and vertical height <u>3 cm</u>.

10) a) If a circle has a <u>diameter of 12 m</u>, what is its <u>radius</u>?
    b) What is the <u>approximate value of</u> π?

11) A plate has a <u>radius of 6 cm</u>. Find its <u>circumference</u>.

12) A prism has a <u>cross-sectional area</u> of <u>55 cm^2</u>, and a <u>length</u> of <u>100 cm</u>.
    Find its <u>volume</u> (don't forget the <u>units</u>).

13) What does it mean if two shapes are:
    a) <u>congruent</u>,   b) <u>similar</u>?

Metric and Imperial Units

Learning this stuff means more than just exam marks.
It can also help you out with old cake recipes where the ingredients are in ounces. Mmm, cake...

Metric Units

You can spot metric units because they often start with things like 'milli' and 'kilo'.

To change between them you have to times or divide by 10, 100, 1000... etc. as shown below.

SOME METRIC UNITS:

1) Length   mm, cm, m, km
2) Area   mm², cm², m², km²
3) Volume   mm³, cm³, m³, litres, ml
4) Mass   g, kg, tonnes

MEMORISE THESE KEY FACTS:

1 cm = 10 mm	1 tonne = 1000 kg
1 m = 100 cm	1 litre = 1000 ml
1 km = 1000 m	1 litre = 1000 cm³
1 kg = 1000 g	1 cm³ = 1 ml

EXAMPLE: My brother is 180 cm tall. How tall is he in a) mm, and b) m?
   a) 1 cm = 10 mm, so 180 cm must be 180 × 10 = 1800 mm.
   b) 100 cm = 1 m, so 180 cm must be 180 ÷ 100 = 1.80 m.

There's more of this over the page so don't panic if you don't quite get it yet.

Imperial Units

Imperial units are 'old style' units. We still use them though (e.g. giving heights in feet and inches).
You don't need to remember these conversions in the exam, but you need to be able to use them.

SOME IMPERIAL UNITS:

1) Length   Inches, feet, yards, miles
2) Area   Square inches, square miles
3) Volume   Cubic feet, gallons, pints
4) Mass   Ounces, pounds, stones, tons

IMPERIAL UNIT CONVERSIONS:

1 Foot = 12 Inches
1 Yard = 3 Feet
1 Gallon = 8 Pints
1 Stone = 14 Pounds (lbs)
1 Pound = 16 Ounces (oz)

EXAMPLE: My dog weighs 2 stones. How many pounds is this?
   1 stone = 14 lbs, so 2 stones must be 2 × 14 = 28 lbs.

Imperial units — they're mint...

Learn the bits in the blue box, then cover the page and try to scribble them all down.

1) a) How many cm is 2 metres?   b) How many mm is 65 cm?
2) a) How many kg is 2000 g?   b) How many litres is 3000 cm³?
3) A rod is 48 inches long. What is this in feet?

Conversion Factors

A <u>conversion factor</u> is just a number that tells you <u>how many times bigger or smaller</u> one thing is compared to another. For example, a kilogram (kg) is 1000 times bigger than a gram (g), so the conversion factor is <u>1000</u>. You can use them to <u>change between different units</u>.

Method

Hmm, seems okay so far. But I tell you what'd really convince me — an example using slugs...

1) Find the <u>CONVERSION FACTOR</u>.
2) <u>Multiply AND divide</u> by the conversion factor.
3) Choose the <u>COMMON SENSE ANSWER</u>.
   (This is just the answer that seems most likely).

Example 1:

See previous page for the conversion factors.

"A Giant Sea-slug called Kevin was washed up near Grange-Over-Sands. He was <u>18.6 m</u> in length. How long is this in <u>cm</u>?"

Step 1)   <u>Find the CONVERSION FACTOR</u>
In this question the Conversion Factor = <u>100</u>
(because 1 m = <u>100</u> cm)

Step 2)   <u>MULTIPLY AND DIVIDE by the conversion factor</u>:
18.6 m × 100 = 1860 cm (seems okay)
18.6 m ÷ 100 = 0.186 cm (way too small)

Step 3)   <u>Choose the COMMON SENSE answer</u>:
The answer is 18.6 m = <u>1860 cm</u>

Example 2:

"Lisa's garden pond holds <u>200 pints</u> of water. How much is this in <u>gallons</u>, if 1 gallon is 8 pints?"

Step 1)   <u>Find the CONVERSION FACTOR</u>
Conversion Factor = <u>8</u>   (because 1 gallon = <u>8</u> pints)

Step 2)   <u>MULTIPLY AND DIVIDE by the conversion factor</u>:
200 pints × 8 = 1600 gallons
200 pints ÷ 8 = 25 gallons

Step 3)   <u>Choose the COMMON SENSE answer</u>:
A gallon must be <u>bigger than a pint</u> if there are 8 pints in a gallon.
So there must be <u>fewer gallons than pints</u> in the pond.
The answer must be 200 pints = <u>25 gallons</u>

Conversion Factors

Example 3:

"A popular item at our local shop is Lumpy Sprout Ketchup (not available in all areas). The Extra Large Size is the most popular and weighs 2400 g. How much is this in kg?"

Step 1) Conversion Factor = 1000
(because 1 kg = 1000 g)

Step 2) 2400 × 1000 = 2 400 000 kg   (Uulp..)
2400 ÷ 1000 = 2.4 kg   (that's more like it)

Step 3) So the answer must be that 2400 g = 2.4 kg

Gimme gimme.

Example 4:

"Toby, my pet elephant, weighs 12 tonnes. How much does he weigh in kg?"

Step 1) Conversion Factor = 1000
(because 1 tonne = 1000 kg)

Step 2) 12 × 1000 = 12 000 kg   (looks OK)
12 ÷ 1000 = 0.012 kg   (that's a pretty light elephant)

Step 3) So the answer must be that 12 tonnes = 12 000 kg

You don't have the Conversion Factor. I thought it was very karaoke...

What a nice feeling — two lovely pages and just the 3 steps of the Conversion Factor method to learn. If you're reading this and you've still no idea what the Conversion Factor method is — look at all the big colourful boxes on the last two pages. Not only are they pretty, they'll help you with these...

1) Kevin the Sea-slug was found to weigh 0.16 tonnes. What is this in kg?

2) My little brother eats 32 ounces of Lumpy Sprout Ketchup per day.
What is this in pounds? (1 pound = 16 ounces).

Rounding Off

Big numbers and decimals are often <u>rounded off</u> in real life. This isn't too bad if you learn the rules.

Rounding Whole Numbers

The main ways to round off a number are:

1) '<u>To the nearest WHOLE NUMBER</u>'
2) '<u>To the nearest TEN</u>'
3) '<u>To the nearest HUNDRED</u>'
4) '<u>To the nearest THOUSAND</u>'

The <u>2 RULES</u> for rounding are:

> 1) The number <u>always lies between 2 POSSIBLE ANSWERS</u>.
>   Just <u>choose the one it's NEAREST TO</u>.
> 2) If the number is <u>exactly in the MIDDLE</u>, then <u>ROUND IT UP</u>.

<u>EXAMPLES</u>:

1) Give 231 to the nearest <u>TEN</u>.

ANSWER: 231 is between 230 and 240, but it is nearer to <u>230</u>

2) Give 145 to the nearest <u>HUNDRED</u>.

ANSWER: 145 is between 100 and 200, but it is nearer to <u>100</u>

3) Round 45.7 to the nearest <u>WHOLE NUMBER</u>.

ANSWER: 45.7 is between 45 and 46, but it is nearer to <u>46</u>

4) Round 4500 to the nearest <u>THOUSAND</u>.

ANSWER: 4500 is between 4000 and 5000. In fact it is exactly halfway
between them. <u>So we ROUND IT UP</u> (see Rule 2 above) to <u>5000</u>

Decimal Places (D.P.)

Rounding off to <u>ONE DECIMAL PLACE</u> (or <u>1 d.p.</u>) means leaving <u>one digit after the decimal point</u>.
Follow the same rules as above but think carefully about the '<u>two possible answers</u>'.

<u>EXAMPLES</u>: Round off 2.34 to 1 decimal place.

<u>ANSWER</u>: 2.34 is between 2.3 and 2.4, but it's nearer to <u>2.3</u>

Round off 4.57 to 1 decimal place.

<u>ANSWER</u>: 4.57 is between 4.5 and 4.6, but nearer to <u>4.6</u>

Round off 2.01 to 1 decimal place.

<u>ANSWER</u>: 2.01 is between 2.0 and 2.1, but nearer to <u>2.0</u>

You still have to include the zero,
otherwise it's not rounded to 1 d.p.

Exam cheat wish #23 — all marks are rounded up to the nearest 100%...

Learn the <u>2 rules for rounding</u> and how to round to <u>one decimal place</u>. Simples.

1) Round these off to the nearest whole number: a) 3.4   b) 5.2   c) 1.84   d) 6.9   e) 3.26
2) Round these numbers off to the nearest hundred: a) 286   b) 450   c) 123
3) Round these to 1 d.p: a) 5.37   b) 0.103

Clock Time Questions

`20:23:47`
`08:23:47`

Times in '24 hour clock' are given as a number between 00.00 (midnight) and 23.59 (11.59 pm). Times in '12 hour clock' are given between 1.00 and 12.59, but need the 'am' and 'pm' bit to say if it's morning or afternoon.

1) am and pm

1) 'am' means 'morning'. It runs from 12 midnight to 12 noon.

2) 'pm' means 'afternoon and evening'. It runs from 12 noon to 12 midnight.

3) For morning times, 24 hour clock and 12 hour clock times are written THE SAME.

4) For afternoon times, ADD 12 HOURS to the 12 hour clock time to get it in 24 hour clock. To go from 24 hour clock to 12 hour clock, TAKE AWAY 12 HOURS (and put 'pm').

5) For example, 2230 in '24 hour clock' is 22.30 – 12.00 = 10.30 pm in '12 hour clock'.

2) Conversions

You'll definitely need to know these important conversions:

EXAMPLE: How many minutes are there in 2.5 hours?

1 hour = 60 minutes, so 2.5 hours is:
2.5 × 60 = 150 minutes.

> 1 day = 24 hours
> 1 hour = 60 minutes
> 1 minute = 60 seconds

3) Exam Questions Involving 'Time'

There's a GOOD METHOD for exam questions about time:

Take your time, write it down, and split it up into SHORT EASY STAGES

EXAMPLE: Find the time taken by a train which sets off at 1325 and arrives at 1910.

Split it into short easy stages like this:

1325 → 1400 → 1900 → 1910
　　35 mins　　5 hours　　10 mins

Then add up the separate parts to find the total time from 1325 to 1910:

5 hours + 35 mins + 10 mins = 5 hours 45 mins.

See page 4 for more on time and timetables.

It feels more like 600 minutes in an hour's maths lesson...

Even if you know lots of this stuff already, the tips are useful — so don't just ignore them.

1) What is 17.15 in 12 hour clock? (don't forget am/pm)

2) How many minutes are there in a day? And how many seconds are there in a day?

3) What is 3.5 hours in hours and minutes? What is 5¾ hours in hours and minutes?

4) A plane sets off at 10.15 am. The flight lasts 5 hrs 50 mins. What is the arrival time?

Compass Directions and Bearings

By the end of this page you should have got your bearings about <u>bearings</u>. Ahem.

The Eight Points Of the Compass

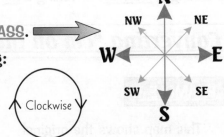

1) Make sure you know all these <u>8 DIRECTIONS ON THE COMPASS</u>.

2) Remember the order of the <u>main 4</u> going <u>clockwise</u> by saying:
"Naughty Elephants Squirt Water".

3) For <u>other directions</u> (i.e. not exactly North or South
or South-East, etc), you have to use <u>BEARINGS</u>.

Bearings

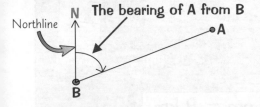

1) A bearing is a <u>DIRECTION</u> given as an <u>ANGLE</u> in degrees.

2) All bearings are measured <u>CLOCKWISE</u> from the <u>NORTHLINE</u>.
(Just a line pointing North.)

3) All bearings are given as <u>3 figures</u>: e.g. 060°
rather than just 60°, 008° rather than 8°, etc.

The 3 Key Words For Bearings Questions

| 1) 'FROM' | Find the word '<u>FROM</u>' in the question, and put your pencil on the diagram at the point you are going '<u>from</u>'. |

> You might need to draw a line between the two points if it's not already there.

| 2) NORTHLINE | At the point you are going '<u>FROM</u>', draw in a <u>NORTHLINE</u>. |

| 3) CLOCKWISE | Now draw in or measure the angle <u>CLOCKWISE</u> from the <u>northline</u> to the line joining the two points. This angle is the <u>BEARING</u>. |

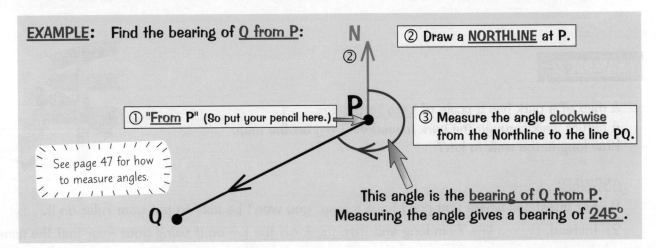

<u>EXAMPLE</u>:   Find the bearing of <u>Q from P</u>:

② Draw a <u>NORTHLINE</u> at P.

① "<u>From</u> P" (So put your pencil here.)

③ Measure the angle <u>clockwise</u> from the Northline to the line PQ.

See page 47 for how to measure angles.

This angle is the <u>bearing of Q from P</u>.
Measuring the angle gives a bearing of <u>245°</u>.

Compasses — we'd be lost without them...

Learn the <u>eight points</u> of a compass, and the <u>3 key words</u> for bearings, and you'll be fine.

1) Draw a blob on a piece of paper to represent home, and then draw a line:
a) going out in a <u>South-Westerly direction</u> from home, and b) <u>on a bearing of 080°</u> from home.

Maps and Map Scales

The most usual map scale is "1 cm = so many km". This just tells you how many km in real life it is for 1 cm measured on the actual map. This is really useful stuff to learn if you're planning a journey, or taking a maths exam any time soon...

Converting "cm on the Map" into "Real km"

EXAMPLE 1:

This map shows the original M6 Motorway built by the Romans in AD120.

The scale of the map is 1 cm to 8 km.

Work out the length of the section of M6 between Wigan and Preston.

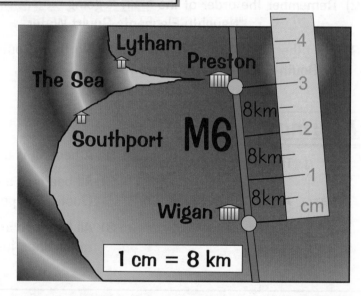

Lytham
Preston
The Sea
8km
Southport M6
8km
8km
Wigan

1 cm = 8 km

ANSWER: as shown on the map:

1) Put your ruler against the bit you're finding the length of.
   Make sure the zero on the ruler is lined up with the starting place (in this case, Wigan).

2) Mark off each whole cm and write next to each one the distance in km.

3) Add up all the km you just marked.
   So between Wigan and Preston: 8 km + 8 km + 8 km = 24 km.

EXAMPLE 2:

A map of a park has a scale of 1 cm to 0.1 km.
A nature walk through the park measures 7 cm on the map.
How long is the walk in km?

Flying Pigs
Sitting Ducks

ANSWER:

1) For questions where you don't have a map, you won't be able to put your ruler on it.

2) Instead, draw a line 7 cm long and then mark off the km on it using your ruler just the same.

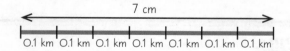

7 cm

0.1 km 0.1 km 0.1 km 0.1 km 0.1 km 0.1 km 0.1 km

3) So the distance is:
   0.1 + 0.1 + 0.1 + 0.1 + 0.1 + 0.1 + 0.1
   = 7 × 0.1 = 0.7 km.

Maps and Map Scales

You also need to know how to work out sizes on a map or scale drawing using the 'real life' size. This is handy if you want to <u>draw something to scale</u>.

Converting "Real km" into "cm on the Map"

EXAMPLE: A map is drawn on a scale of <u>1 cm to 2 km</u>.
If a road is <u>12 km</u> long in real life, how long will it be in <u>cm</u> on the map?

ANSWER:

1) Start by drawing the road as a <u>straight line</u>:

2) Mark off each <u>cm</u> and fill in <u>how many km it is</u> for each one:

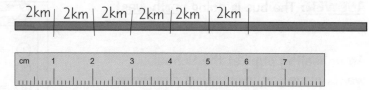

3) Keep going <u>until the km add up to the full distance</u>. (12 km in this case.)

4) Then just <u>count how many cms long your line is</u> — in this case it's <u>6 cm</u>.

It Works For Other Scales Too

EXAMPLE: Larry wants to draw a picture of his robot, Barry, to a scale of <u>1 cm to 20 cm</u>.
How tall will Barry be on the drawing if he is <u>80 cm</u> tall in real life?

ANSWER:

1) Draw the height as a <u>straight line</u>.

2) Mark off each <u>cm</u> and fill in <u>how many 'real life' cm it is</u>.

3) Keep going <u>until you get the full height</u>. (80 cm.)

4) <u>Count how many cms long your line is</u> — in this case it's <u>4 cm</u>.

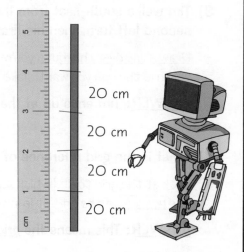

What's the king of the pencil case?

The ruler... Sorry... Right, have a go at these:

1) Work out the length in metres of the runway shown here: ——————➤

2) How many cm on the map would a 600 m runway be? (HINT: use the scale shown on the map).

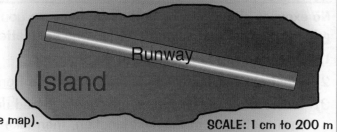

SCALE: 1 cm to 200 m

Section Three — Measurements

Maps and Directions

Being able to read a map and follow <u>directions</u> is a very, very useful skill...

Map References <u>and</u> Directions

EXAMPLES:

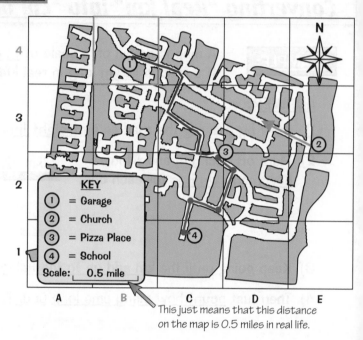

1) A bus drives from the Church to the Garage. Is it travelling north-west or north-east?

   <u>Draw an arrow</u> to show the direction you want to find. Compare the <u>Northline</u> with <u>your line</u>.

   <u>ANSWER</u>: **The bus is going <u>north-west</u>.**

2) An unhealthy pupil at the School wants pizza for lunch. Give directions from the school to the Pizza Place.

   <u>Draw a line over the route</u> you want to describe, and <u>put a big blob at each turn-off</u>. Remember to state the <u>direction of turn</u>, and which <u>number turn</u> it is:

   <u>ANSWER</u>: **Turn <u>right</u> out of the school and take the <u>first right</u>. Take the <u>second left</u> then take the <u>first left</u>. The Pizza Place is on the <u>right</u>.**

This just means that this distance on the map is 0.5 miles in real life.

3) Tim walks south-east from the Garage and takes the third right turn. He then takes the second left turn, then his first left and walks to the next junction. Where is he?

   <u>Draw a line over the route</u> you're following. <u>Carefully count each turn</u> you go past so you know which is the one you want. Take the turn, and <u>do the same again</u>.

   <u>ANSWER</u>: **Tim ends up at the <u>Pizza Place</u>.**

4) What is the grid reference of the Garage?

   Look at the grid to find which square it is in. <u>Firstly</u> (and the order is <u>very important</u>), go along the <u>bottom</u> of the grid. It is in column B. <u>THEN</u> look <u>up the side</u> of the grid. It is in row 4.

   <u>ANSWER</u>: **This means the <u>grid reference is B4</u>.**

This page will help you make your way to the exam...

No excuses about missing your exam because you got lost. To remember the order for <u>grid references</u>, just say <u>FAT</u> Uncle. The bold letters mean <u>First Across, Then Up</u>.

1) What is the grid reference of the School?
2) What compass direction is the Pizza Place <u>from</u> the Garage?
3) Where do these directions take you? "Head due west from the Pizza Place. Take the third left turn, turn eastwards at the next junction, then take the second right. Turn left at the dead-end."

Speed

Speed is <u>how fast</u> something's moving. You need to know the speed formula <u>and</u> how to use it.
Luckily there's a <u>formula triangle</u> on hand to help.

Speed = Distance ÷ Time

1) To work out how <u>fast</u> something's going, you need
   to know the <u>time</u> taken to go a certain <u>distance</u>.

2) Then use the <u>formula</u>:

$$\text{Speed} = \text{Distance} \div \text{Time}$$

> <u>EXAMPLE</u>: If I take 2 hours to walk 8 miles, what is my speed?
> <u>ANSWER</u>: Speed = distance ÷ time = 8 miles ÷ 2 hours = <u>4 miles per hour</u> (mph).

Use the Triangle for Distance and Time

1) You might be <u>given the speed</u> of something and be asked to find:
   a) the <u>distance</u> it travels in a certain time   <u>OR</u>   b) the <u>time</u> it takes to go a certain distance.

2) These problems are <u>loads easier</u> with this <u>formula triangle</u>.

3) To <u>use</u> the triangle, just <u>cover up</u> the letter of the thing you're after,
   then <u>what's left</u> is the <u>formula</u> you need.

4) For example, to get the formula for '<u>distance</u>', cover up the '<u>D</u>'.
   This leaves you with '<u>S × T</u>', so the formula is <u>D = S × T</u>
   (Distance = Speed × Time).

5) You need to <u>LEARN</u> where the letters go in this triangle
   — they won't give it to you in the exam.

> <u>EXAMPLE</u>:   A car travels <u>90 miles</u> at <u>30 miles per hour</u>.
>   How long does it take?
> <u>ANSWER</u>:   <u>We want to find the TIME</u>,
>   so <u>cover up T</u> in the triangle which leaves $\frac{D}{S}$.
>   So   <u>T = D ÷ S</u>
>   Time = Distance ÷ speed = 90 ÷ 30 = <u>3 hours</u>

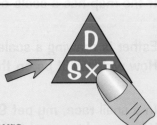

Formula triangles — it's all a big cover up...

Formula triangles are the <u>most useful thing ever</u>. They make remembering things like the speed formula
<u>much easier</u>. Learn the whole page, cover it up, and write down the formula triangle for speed.

Revision Test for Section Three

1) Ali's pet worm is <u>6 cm</u> long. How long is this in: a) <u>millimetres</u>, b) <u>metres</u>?

2) Jane is making pancakes. She has <u>0.7 litres</u> of milk but the recipe says she needs <u>600 cm³</u>. Does she have enough milk to make the pancakes?

3) Joe's bed is <u>4 feet wide</u>. His blanket is <u>50 inches</u> wide. Which is <u>wider</u>?

4) Kylie is going on holiday and needs some spending money. She wants to take <u>$2400</u>. How much is that in <u>pounds</u> (£), if <u>£1 = $12</u>?

This is a conversion factor question.

5) These are the sort of numbers you might get in your <u>calculator display</u>:
a) 1.2343534   b) 2.9999999   c) 15.534624   d) 12.0833
<u>Round them off</u> to the <u>nearest whole number</u>.

6) a) Round 246 to the <u>nearest 10</u>.   b) Round 860 to the <u>nearest 100</u>.

7) Round these numbers off to <u>1 decimal place</u>:   a) 5.32   b) 3.46   c) 6.15

8) John's train leaves the station at <u>1.15 pm</u>. He knows it takes him <u>25 mins</u> to walk to the station. What is the <u>latest time</u> he should leave the house?

9) A film is <u>190 minutes</u> long. It starts at <u>18.15</u>. What time will it finish in:
a) 24 hour clock time,   b) 12 hour clock time?

10) Draw a diagram showing the <u>eight points</u> of the compass.

11) A ship sets off from Port P on a <u>bearing of 160°</u>.
<u>Show its direction</u> on the drawing opposite:

Port P

12) Jeb is planning a road trip. On the map his journey measures <u>12 cm</u>.
If the map has a scale of <u>1 cm to 30 km</u>, what is the real length of his journey in km?

13) Esther is drawing a scale plan of her bedroom, which is <u>6 m wide</u>.
How wide will it be on the drawing if she uses a scale of <u>1 cm to 0.5 m</u>?

14) In a snail race, my pet Slimy finished the <u>2 metre</u> race in <u>200 seconds</u>.
What was his <u>speed</u> in metres per second (m/s)?

15) Laura is planning a walk in the countryside. The route she has planned is <u>15 km</u> long.
Laura knows that she walks at an average speed of <u>5 km/h</u>.
a) How <u>long</u> will the walk take, in <u>hours</u>?
b) When will she <u>finish</u> if she sets off at 10.18?

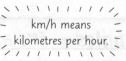
km/h means kilometres per hour.

Lines and Angles

Angles aren't <u>that</u> bad — you just have to <u>learn</u> them, that's all. And sometimes give them sweets.

The <u>Four</u> Types of Angle

1) <u>Acute</u> Angles

<u>SHARP POINTY ONES:</u>
(less than 90 degrees (90°))

2) <u>Obtuse</u> Angles

<u>FLATTER-LOOKING ONES:</u>
(between 90° and 180°)

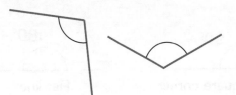

3) <u>Reflex</u> Angles

<u>ONES THAT BEND BACK
ON THEMSELVES:</u>
(more than 180°)

4) <u>Right</u> Angles

<u>SQUARE CORNERS</u>
(exactly 90°)

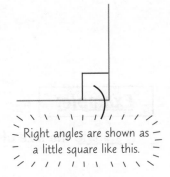

~ Right angles are shown as ~
~ a little square like this. ~

Angles Are Named Using <u>Three</u> Letters

1) In most angle questions, the diagram will have a <u>letter</u> next to each <u>corner</u>.

2) To say which angle you're talking about, use <u>THREE of the letters</u>.

3) The <u>MIDDLE LETTER</u> is the corner <u>where the angle is</u>.

4) The <u>OTHER TWO LETTERS</u> tell you <u>WHICH TWO LINES</u> are <u>either side</u> of the angle.

EXAMPLES:

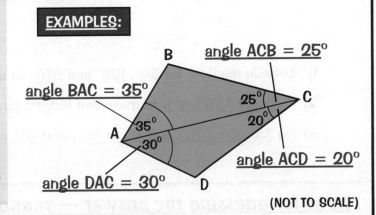

angle ACB = 25°
angle BAC = 35°
angle ACD = 20°
angle DAC = 30°

(NOT TO SCALE)

<u>Roses are red, tulips are plum, if you were an angle you'd be acute one...</u>

Ho, ho, ho — pretty funny aren't I. Anyway, moving on...

1) **LEARN** what **ACUTE, OBTUSE, REFLEX** and **RIGHT ANGLES** are. Draw one example of each.

Lines and Angles

Sometimes you can be asked to <u>estimate</u> the size of an angle.
An estimate is just a <u>clever guess</u>, and there are a few tricks to help you guess it <u>right</u>.

Estimating Angles

1) You need to <u>KNOW THESE FOUR SPECIAL ANGLES</u> off by heart:

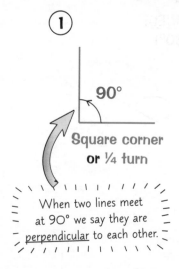

① 90°
Square corner
or ¼ turn

② 180°
Flat line
or ½ turn

③ 270°
¾ turn

④ 360°
Full turn

When two lines meet
at 90° we say they are
<u>perpendicular</u> to each other.

2) You can then <u>compare another angle</u> to the <u>main four</u>
and decide <u>how much BIGGER OR SMALLER</u> it is.

3) E.g. if an angle looks like it's <u>halfway between 90° and 180°</u>, then it's
probably <u>around 135°</u> (because 135 is halfway between 90 and 180).

Don't mix this up with
<u>measuring angles</u> — that's
covered on the next page.

Example:

<u>Estimate</u> the size of these three angles A, B and C:

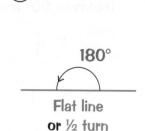 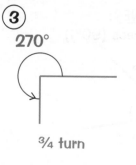 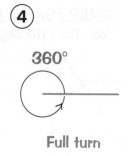

90°

A

90°

B

180°

270°

C

1) Draw in the <u>lines</u> for <u>90°</u>, <u>180°</u> and <u>270°</u> as shown.

2) <u>Compare A, B and C</u> to these and judge <u>how much BIGGER OR SMALLER</u> they are.

3) So <u>A is about 70°</u>, <u>B is about 110°</u>, and <u>C is about 260°</u>.

Marks for guessing the answer — sounds like my kind of question...

OK, so you won't actually get any marks just for guessing — you need to make a good guess.
Better practise then...

1) Estimate these angles:

a) 45°

b) 80°

c) 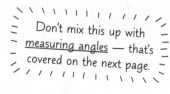 70°

d) 280°

Measuring Angles with Protractors

You might be asked to give the <u>exact value</u> of an angle rather than an estimate.
<u>DON'T PANIC</u>, just reach for your <u>protractor</u> and follow the tips below.

Two Rules for Getting it Right

There are <u>TWO REALLY IMPORTANT THINGS</u> to watch out for when using a <u>protractor</u>:

> 1) <u>ALWAYS put the 0° LINE</u> at the <u>START OF THE ANGLE</u>.
>
> 2) <u>CHECK</u> you're reading from the <u>RIGHT SCALE</u>.

These scales won't work.

How To Measure An Angle:

1) <u>ALWAYS</u> position the protractor with the <u>0° line</u> along the start line of the angle, as shown here:

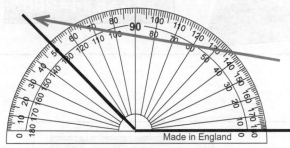

2) <u>COUNT THE ANGLE IN 10° STEPS</u> from the <u>0° line</u> right round to the <u>other one</u> over there.

←Start line (0°)

3) <u>BEFORE YOU READ A NUMBER OFF THE SCALE</u> — check it's the <u>RIGHT SCALE</u> first, because there are <u>TWO scales to choose from</u>.

4) The answer here is <u>130°</u> — <u>NOT 50°</u>. You should get this right if you start <u>counting</u> 10°, 20°, 30°, 40°, etc. <u>from the start line</u> until you reach the other line.

5) You could also <u>estimate</u> it as a check. It looks like an <u>obtuse angle</u> so it must be <u>between 90° and 180°</u> (see p. 45) — which means <u>130° is the right number</u> to pick.

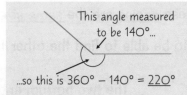

This angle measured
to be 140°...

...so this is 360° – 140° = <u>220°</u>

For <u>reflex angles</u> (see p. 45) like this one — measure the angle on the <u>OTHER SIDE</u> then <u>take it away from 360°</u>.

Neither will these.

See how you measure up when it comes to angles...

...and have a go at these:

1) LEARN the 2 rules for using protractors. Close the book and say them to yourself.
2) Use a protractor to measure angles a), b), c) and d) at the bottom of page 46.

Five Angle Rules

Rules, rules, rules. You've got to love them. Or at least learn them.
Try these 5 simple rules for size:

1) Angles in a triangle

Add up to 180°.

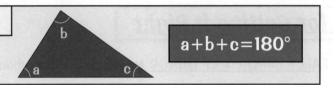

$$a+b+c=180°$$

2) Angles on a straight line

Add up to 180°.

$$a+b+c=180°$$

3) Angles in a 4-sided shape

(a 'quadrilateral')
Add up to 360°.

$$a+b+c+d=360°$$

4) Angles round a point

Add up to 360°.

$$a+b+c+d=360°$$

5) Isosceles triangles

2 sides the same
2 angles the same

These lines mean the two
sides are the same length...

...which means these angles are the same size.

In an isosceles triangle, <u>YOU ONLY NEED TO KNOW ONE ANGLE</u> to be able to find the other two.

a)
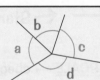

180° − 40° = 140° (see rule 1 above)
<u>The two bottom angles are both
the same</u> and they must add up to
140°, so each one must be <u>half</u> of
140°. So x = 140° ÷ 2 = <u>70°</u>.

b)

The <u>two bottom angles
must be the same</u>, so
50° + 50° = 100°.
All the angles add up to 180°
so y = 180° − 100° = <u>80°</u>.

Parallel and Perpendicular Lines

Up next — <u>parallel</u> and <u>perpendicular</u> lines.
The <u>names</u> may sound scary, but if you learn the next <u>two pages</u> then you're off to a good start.

Angles and Lines

Perpendicular Lines

1) If two lines cross at <u>90°</u> (<u>right-angles</u>)
   they're called <u>perpendicular lines</u>.

2) Mark on the right angle using a <u>little square</u>, like so:

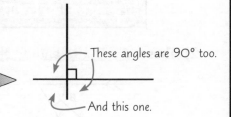

These angles are 90° too.

And this one.

Parallel Lines

1) <u>Parallel lines</u> are lines that will <u>never meet</u>,
   no matter how far you stretch them out.
   They always stay the <u>same distance apart</u>.

2) Parallel lines are usually marked with <u>little arrows</u>, like this:

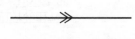

The arrows mean these
2 lines are parallel.

3) When a line cuts across <u>2 parallel lines</u>, it makes two
   <u>bunches of angles</u> which are the <u>same</u>, as shown below:

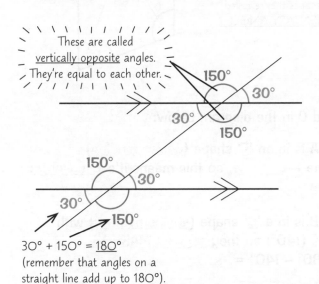

These are called
<u>vertically opposite</u> angles.
They're equal to each other.

150° 30°
30° 150°

150° 30°
30° 150°

30° + 150° = <u>180°</u>
(remember that angles on a
straight line add up to 180°).

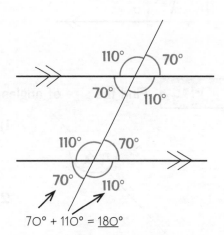

110° 70°
70° 110°

110° 70°
70° 110°

70° + 110° = <u>180°</u>

<u>INSIDE THE BUNCHES OF ANGLES:</u>

- there are <u>only two different angles</u>: <u>A SMALLER ONE</u> and <u>A BIGGER ONE</u>.

- the bigger angle and the smaller angle <u>ALWAYS ADD UP TO 180°</u>.

   (E.g. <u>30° and 150°</u> or <u>70° and 110°</u> in the examples above.)

Parallel and Perpendicular Lines

The hardest bit about angles around parallel lines is <u>spotting them in the first place</u>.
Once you've done that, you can have fun <u>working out what the angles are</u>. Well, I say '<u>fun</u>'...

Angles *Between* Parallel Lines

1) When you have a line <u>crossing a pair of parallel lines</u>, loads of the angles are either

> **THE SAME AS EACH OTHER**   OR   **ADD TOGETHER TO MAKE 180°**

2) These '<u>Z', 'C', 'U' and 'F' shapes</u> will tell you which angles do what:

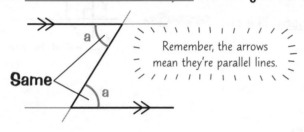

Same

Remember, the arrows
mean they're parallel lines.

In a <u>Z-shape</u> they're called
<u>ALTERNATE ANGLES</u>

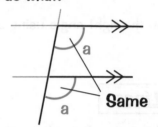

a

a

Same

In an <u>F-shape</u> they're called
<u>CORRESPONDING ANGLES</u>

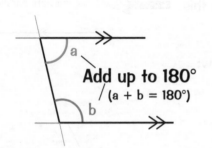

a

Add up to 180°
(a + b = 180°)

b

If they add up to 180°, like in the
C and U shapes they're called
<u>SUPPLEMENTARY ANGLES</u>

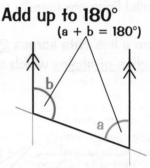

Add up to 180°
(a + b = 180°)

b

a

EXAMPLE: Find the <u>size</u> of angles A, B and C in the diagram below:

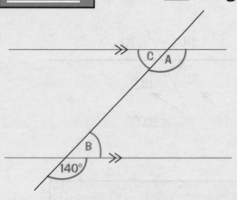

1) Angle A is in an '<u>F</u>' shape (<u>corresponding</u>)
with the <u>140° angle</u>, so this means it's <u>THE SAME</u>:
<u>A = 140°</u>.

2) Angle B is in a '<u>C</u>' shape (<u>supplementary</u>) with
<u>angle A</u> (140°) so they <u>ADD TO MAKE 180°</u>:
<u>B</u> = 180° – 140° = <u>40°</u>.

3) Angle 'C' is in a '<u>Z</u>' shape (<u>alternate</u>) with <u>angle B</u>
(40°) so this means it's <u>THE SAME</u>: <u>C = 40°</u>.

Parallel line spotting — not the coolest of hobbies...

Spotting parallel lines is really, <u>really</u> important, so always have a good look for them.
You don't want to miss them. Have a practice with this:

1) The diagram shown here has one angle given as 60°. Find all the <u>other 7 angles</u>.

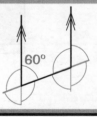

60°

Section Four — Angles and Geometry

The Four Transformations — Translation

Shapes can be <u>transformed</u> (changed) by changing their <u>position</u> or <u>size</u>, <u>spinning</u> or <u>reflecting</u> them. There are <u>four types</u> of <u>transformation</u> — let's kick things off with a look at <u>translation</u>.

Translation means Sliding

1) A <u>translation</u> is just a <u>SLIDE</u>.
   The shape just slides to <u>another place</u>.

2) You have to say <u>how far along</u> and <u>how far up or down</u> the shape has moved.

3) You'll often be given shapes on a <u>grid</u> like the one below.

4) You have to say <u>how many squares</u> along and how many up or down a shape has moved.

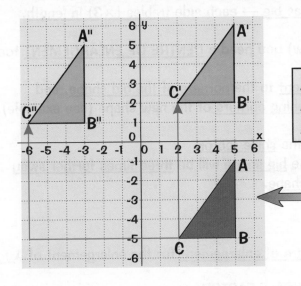

EXAMPLES:
ABC to A'B'C' is a <u>translation</u> of <u>7 up</u>.
ABC to A''B''C'' is a <u>translation</u> of <u>8 left and 6 up</u>.

It helps if you just look at how one corner of the shape has moved. The arrows show how <u>corner C</u> has moved <u>7 squares up</u> for the first translation, and <u>8 squares left and 6 up</u> for the second one.

Give Your Answer in the Right Form

1) To get marks in the exam, you need to give translations in what's known as '<u>vector form</u>'.

2) This looks like a pair of <u>coordinates</u> (see page 75) '<u>standing up</u>':

> The <u>top</u> number '<u>x</u>' is the number of spaces <u>right</u>.
> The <u>bottom</u> number '<u>y</u>' is the number of spaces <u>up</u>.
> $\begin{pmatrix} x \rightarrow \\ \uparrow y \end{pmatrix}$

If the shape has moved <u>left</u> or <u>down</u>, just use <u>negative numbers</u>.

3) For example, '<u>7 up</u>' is just $\begin{pmatrix} 0 \\ 7 \end{pmatrix}$, because there's <u>no movement</u> left or right.

4) A translation of <u>8 left</u> and <u>6 up</u> is written: $\begin{pmatrix} -8 \\ 6 \end{pmatrix}$.

Don't get lost in translation...

When you're trying to see how far <u>up and along</u> a shape has moved, just focus on <u>one</u> of the corners to see where its 'matching' corner has moved to. Same goes if you're trying to <u>draw</u> a translated shape. Just move each point on the shape <u>one at a time</u>, then join the dots to finish the new shape.

The Four Transformations — Enlargement

Enlargement is just making something B I G **G E R**.

Shapes Are Enlarged By a Scale Factor

To describe an enlargement
you must know 2 things:

> 1) The SCALE FACTOR
> 2) The CENTRE OF ENLARGEMENT

1) The SCALE FACTOR is how many times bigger the new shape is than the old shape.

2) E.g. a scale factor of 3 makes it three times as big — each side trebles (×3) in length.

3) For enlargements on a grid (like the one below) you need a CENTRE OF ENLARGEMENT too.

4) If you draw lines from the centre of enlargement to the corners of the old shape, and stretch them out, they should touch the matching corners of the new shape (see example).

5) The length of the stretched lines depends on the scale factor.
E.g. for a scale factor of 3, each corner of the big shape will be three times further away from the centre of enlargement as the small shape.

| Example: | Find the scale factor and centre of enlargement for the enlargement of A to B. |

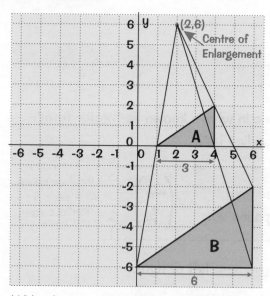

With enlargement, the angles of the two shapes are
the same — they're similar (see p. 32).
The size and position of the shapes are different.

1) **SCALE FACTOR:**

Compare side lengths of the two shapes.

A has a base of 3, and B has a base of 6.

This means B is twice as big as A (6 ÷ 3 = 2)
so the scale factor is 2.

2) **CENTRE OF ENLARGEMENT:**

Join up the corners of B to the matching corners
of A, and stretch out the lines until they meet.

The point where they meet is the centre of
enlargement — here it's at (2,6).

> A to B is an enlargement of
> scale factor 2, centre (2,6).

Go on — supersize me...

It's easy to spot an enlargement — it's the only one of the four transformations that changes the size
of a shape. You've got to know how to find the scale factor and centre of enlargement too though.

The Four Transformations — Rotation

Two down, two to go... A <u>rotation turns a shape around</u>.

You Need to Know 3 Things For Rotation

As well as spotting that a shape has been <u>rotated</u>,
you need to give these <u>3 details</u>:

1) The <u>ANGLE</u> it's been turned by.
2) The <u>DIRECTION</u> of the turn
   (Clockwise or Anticlockwise).
3) The <u>CENTRE OF ROTATION</u>
   — the point it's been turned '<u>about</u>'.

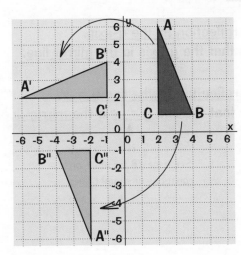

<u>EXAMPLES</u>:

ABC to A'B'C' is a rotation of:
<u>90°</u>, <u>anticlockwise</u>, <u>ABOUT the origin (0,0)</u>.

ABC to A"B"C" is a rotation of:
<u>half a turn (180°)</u>, <u>clockwise</u>, <u>ABOUT the origin (0,0)</u>.

(For half-turns, it doesn't actually matter
if you go clockwise or anticlockwise.)

Use Tracing Paper To Check

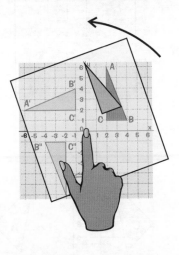

Tracing paper can help with rotations:

1) <u>Trace around</u> the old shape.

2) <u>Hold</u> the tracing paper at the <u>centre of rotation</u>
   (just put your finger there).

3) <u>Spin</u> the tracing paper round, by the <u>angle</u> and <u>direction</u>
   given, and check that the tracing <u>lines up</u> with the new shape.

This page makes me dizzy...

Rotations can sometimes be trickier to spot than the other three transformations. So, if it doesn't look like any of the <u>others</u>, chances are it's a <u>rotation</u>. Don't forget to give all <u>three details</u>.

The Four Transformations — Reflection

Last one now... A <u>reflection</u> is just a <u>mirror image</u>. You have to say <u>where</u> the mirror is though.

Give The <u>Mirror Line</u> <u>For</u> Reflections

> 1) If a shape has been <u>REFLECTED</u>, you only need to say where the <u>MIRROR LINE</u> is.
>
> 2) Each corner of the new shape will be the <u>SAME DISTANCE AWAY</u> from the <u>mirror line</u> as the <u>matching corner</u> of the old shape.

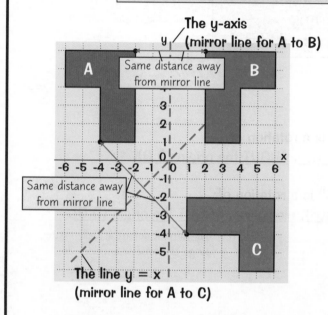

The y-axis
(mirror line for A to B)

Same distance away from mirror line

Same distance away from mirror line

The line y = x
(mirror line for A to C)

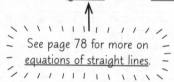
EXAMPLES:

A to B is a <u>reflection IN the y-axis</u>.
This means that the <u>y-axis</u> is the <u>mirror line</u>.

A to C is a <u>reflection IN the line y = x</u>.
This means that the line <u>y = x</u> is the <u>mirror line</u>.

See page 78 for more on <u>equations of straight lines</u>.

Tracing Paper <u>Helps With Reflections</u>

<u>Tracing paper</u> sure is useful stuff...

1) Trace around the <u>old shape</u> and along the <u>mirror line</u>.

2) <u>Flip the tracing paper over</u> and <u>line up the mirror lines</u>.

3) The drawing of the old shape on the tracing paper should <u>line up</u> with the new shape.

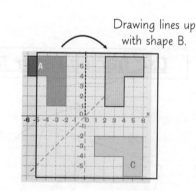
Drawing lines up with shape B.

<u>Time to reflect on the last few pages...</u>

That's all four transformations done. Hurrah. Before you move on:
<u>LEARN the names</u> of the <u>four transformations</u> and the details for each.
Then, when you think you know it, <u>turn over and see what you've learnt</u>.
Finally, do a dance to celebrate. Any dance will do.

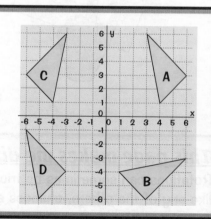

1) Describe <u>fully</u> these 4 transformations:

    A to B,   B to C,   C to A,   A to D.

Use tracing paper to help you.

Constructing Triangles

You need to know how to draw triangles <u>accurately</u> — which means <u>lengths and angles</u> being <u>exactly</u> what they're supposed to be. How you do it depends on <u>what you're told</u> about the triangle...

Three Sides — <u>Use a Ruler and Compasses</u>

When drawing shapes, <u>construct</u> means you have to draw them <u>accurately</u>.

> If you're told <u>all 3 side lengths</u> of the triangle, without knowing the <u>angles</u>, you need a <u>RULER</u> and a <u>PAIR OF COMPASSES</u>.

Example: Construct the triangle ABC where AB = 6 cm, BC = 4 cm, AC = 5 cm.

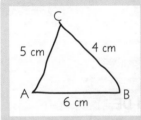

1) First, <u>sketch and label</u> a triangle so you know roughly what's needed.

2) Draw your <u>base line</u> — here it's <u>AB</u>. Draw a line <u>6 cm</u> long and <u>label</u> the ends A and B.

3) For AC, set the <u>compasses</u> to <u>5 cm</u>, put the point at A and <u>draw an arc</u>.

4) For BC, set the compasses to <u>4 cm</u>, put the point at B and <u>draw an arc</u>.

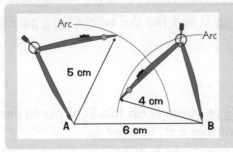

5) Where the <u>arcs cross</u> is the <u>point C</u>.

6) Draw a <u>line</u> from <u>A to C</u> and <u>another</u> <u>line</u> from <u>B to C</u> to finish your triangle.

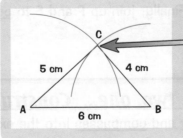

<u>DON'T</u> rub out the arcs — these are your <u>construction lines</u> to show you've done it properly. Make sure you do them lightly in the first place so it's not too messy.

Constructing Triangles

Sides and Angles — Use a Ruler and Protractor

> If you're told 2 side lengths of the triangle, and the angle between them, you need a RULER and a PROTRACTOR.

Example: Construct triangle DEF. DE = 5 cm, DF = 3 cm, and angle EDF = 40°.

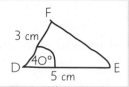

1) Roughly sketch and label the triangle.

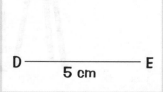

2) Draw the base line — here I've picked DE. Draw a line 5 cm long and label the ends D and E.

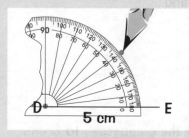

3) Next you have to draw the angle EDF at point D:

- Place the centre of the protractor over D, with the 0° line level with DE.
- Measure 40° and put a dot, as shown.
- Join up D and the dot with a light pencil line.

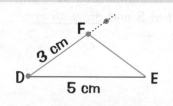

4) Measure 3 cm from D on this light pencil line and put another dot, labelled F.

5) Join up D and F with a thicker line. Now you've drawn the two sides and the angle.

6) Finally, join up F and E to complete the triangle.

Compasses at the ready — three, two, one... Construct...

Don't forget to take a pencil, ruler, protractor and compasses into the exam.

1) Construct a triangle with sides 3 cm, 4 cm and 5 cm. Then check it by measuring the sides.

2) A triangle ABC has sides AB = 8 cm, AC = 5 cm and angle BAC = 49°. Construct the triangle. Measure side BC with a ruler. How long is BC?

Revision Test for Section Four

1) Look at the diagram on the right, and say whether the
following angles are <u>acute</u>, <u>obtuse</u>, <u>reflex</u> or <u>right angles</u>:
   a) **XYZ**
   b) **WZY**
   c) **WXY**
   d) **XWZ**

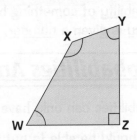

2) <u>Estimate</u> each of the angles below and then <u>measure</u> them.
Make sure your two answers are similar for each angle:

   a)   b)   c)   d)

3) Work out the <u>missing angle</u> inside the <u>quadrilateral</u> on the right.

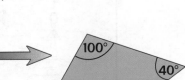

4) Work out <u>angles X and Y</u> in the diagram below:

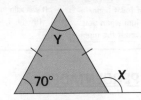

> Use some of the 'five angle rules'
> to help with questions 3 and 4.

5) a) What is the <u>size</u> of <u>angle b</u> in the diagram on the right?
   b) What is the <u>special name</u> given to a pair of angles like a and b?

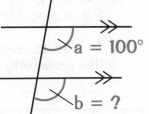

6) What <u>transformation</u> maps
   a) shape A onto shape B?
   b) shape C onto shape D?
   c) shape C onto shape E?

> Make sure you give all
> the details needed for
> each transformation.

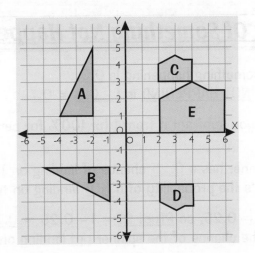

7) <u>Construct a triangle</u> ABC with sides AB = 9 cm, AC = 10 cm and BC = 8 cm.

Probability

The <u>probability</u> of something happening (an '<u>event</u>') is <u>how likely</u> it is to happen.
Probability is given a <u>number</u>, so we can do loads of lovely maths with it. Hurrah.

All Probabilities Are Between 0 and 1

1) Probabilities can only have values <u>from 0 to 1</u> (including 0 and 1).

2) You should be able to put the probability of <u>any event</u> happening on this <u>scale of 0 to 1</u>.

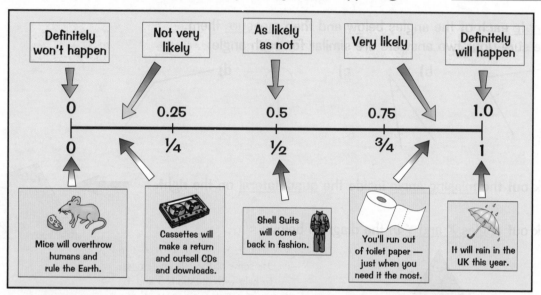

| Definitely won't happen | Not very likely | As likely as not | Very likely | Definitely will happen |

| 0 | 0.25 | 0.5 | 0.75 | 1.0 |
| 0 | ¼ | ½ | ¾ | 1 |

Mice will overthrow humans and rule the Earth.

Cassettes will make a return and outsell CDs and downloads.

Shell Suits will come back in fashion.

You'll run out of toilet paper — just when you need it the most.

It will rain in the UK this year.

3) You can give probabilities using <u>FRACTIONS</u>, <u>DECIMALS</u> or <u>PERCENTAGES</u>.
    E.g. a <u>probability</u> of ½ can also be written as <u>0.5</u> or <u>50%</u>.

4) To <u>save on words</u>, we can write e.g:
    'the <u>probability</u> of tossing a coin and getting a <u>head</u> is <u>0.5</u>' as: <u>P(H) = 0.5</u>.

P is for <u>probability</u>
H is for <u>head</u>

The Probability Of Something Not Happening = 1 – P

1) If the probability of something happening is <u>0.3</u>,
    then the chance of it <u>NOT HAPPENING</u> is <u>1 – 0.3 = 0.7</u>.

2) It's what's left when you <u>subtract it from 1</u> (or 100% for percentages).

<u>EXAMPLE:</u>   A spinner has a <u>0.25</u> chance of landing on <u>TWO</u>.
                  What's the probability of it <u>NOT</u> landing on two?

<u>ANSWER:</u>   <u>P(2) = 0.25</u>, so <u>P(not 2) = 1 – 0.25 = 0.75</u>.
                  So, the chance of the spinner <u>not</u> landing on two is <u>0.75</u>.

P(2) means the probability of getting a 2.

This is probably my favourite topic...

It's <u>very likely</u> that you'll get a question on probability in the exam, so <u>learn this page</u> and answer these:
1) The probability of the local roller derby team winning a match is ¾.
   a) Are they likely or unlikely to win?   b) What is the probability of them <u>NOT</u> winning?

Equal and Unequal Probabilities

It's all <u>fun and games</u> on this page. And a bit of <u>maths</u>. Oh yes.

Equal Probabilities

1) When the different results or '<u>outcomes</u>' of something happening all have
   the <u>same chance of happening</u>, then the probabilities will be <u>EQUAL</u>.

2) These are the <u>two cases</u> which usually come up in exams:

> 1) <u>TOSSING A COIN:</u>   <u>Equal chance</u> of getting a <u>head</u>
>   or a <u>tail</u> (probability = $\frac{1}{2}$)
>
> 2) <u>THROWING A DICE:</u>   <u>Equal chance</u> of getting <u>any</u> of
>   the <u>numbers</u> (probability = $\frac{1}{6}$)

I hope they don't ask me to toss this.

3) Notice that the probability depends on the <u>number of possible outcomes</u>.
   E.g. there are <u>6 different ways</u> a dice can land, so the probability
   of <u>any one of them</u> is '1 out of 6' or $\frac{1}{6}$.

Unequal Probabilities

In most cases, <u>different outcomes</u> have <u>different probabilities</u> — some are <u>more likely</u> than others.

> <u>EXAMPLE 1:</u> "A bag contains 6 blue balls, 5 red balls and 9 green balls. Find P(green)."
>
> <u>ANSWER:</u> The chances of picking out the three colours are <u>NOT EQUAL</u>
> because there are <u>different numbers of balls</u> in each colour.
> The probability of picking a <u>green</u> is:
>
> $$P(green) = \frac{NUMBER\ OF\ GREENS}{TOTAL\ NUMBER\ OF\ BALLS} = \frac{9}{20}$$

> <u>EXAMPLE 2:</u> "What is the probability of winning £45 on this spinner?"
>
> <u>ANSWER:</u>
> The pointer has <u>the same chance</u> of stopping on <u>every sector</u>.
> There are <u>2 out of 8</u> which say £45, so:
>
> $$P(£45) = \frac{2}{8} = \frac{1}{4} \text{ (as a fraction)}$$
> or <u>0.25</u> (as a decimal)
> or <u>25%</u> (as a percentage)

See page 16 for how to swap between fractions, decimals and percentages.

It's enough to make your head spin...

Spinners and bags of balls come up a lot in the exam. Don't panic if they use <u>another example</u> —
you work it out in <u>exactly the same way</u>. Try this one: 1) What is the probability of picking a white
puppy from a bag containing 3 black puppies, 4 brown puppies, 2 white puppies and one purple puppy?

Listing Outcomes

The key to working out probabilities is finding the <u>number of outcomes</u>.
But sometimes it's not clear straight away just <u>how many</u> different outcomes there are.

Listing All Outcomes: Use a Sample Space

1) You might get asked to list <u>all the possible outcomes</u> for <u>TWO THINGS HAPPENING TOGETHER</u>.
A <u>simple</u> question might be to <u>list all the possible results</u> from <u>tossing two coins</u>:

Here H is for heads and T is for tails.

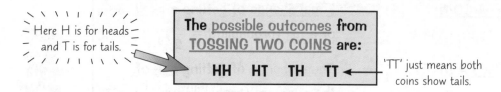

The <u>possible outcomes</u> from <u>TOSSING TWO COINS</u> are:

HH   HT   TH   TT

'TT' just means both coins show tails.

2) You can work out <u>probabilities</u> from your list.
E.g. P(TT) = $\frac{1}{4}$, because there are <u>4 outcomes in total</u>, and <u>only 1 of these is TT</u>.

3) For harder questions, you're better off listing all the possible results in a
<u>sample space diagram</u> — a posh name for a <u>table</u>.

4) The sample space for <u>spinning these two spinners</u> is shown below:

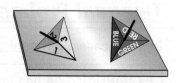

	Red	Blue	Green
1	1R	1B	1G
2	2R	2B	2G
3	3R	3B	3G

3 different outcomes on colour spinner.

3 different outcomes on number spinner.

5) <u>Any number</u> on the number spinner could come up with <u>any colour</u> on the colour spinner.
Spinning them together gives <u>3 × 3 = 9 different combinations altogether</u>.
The sample space is a <u>list</u> of these <u>9 outcomes</u>.

6) The probability of spinning e.g. a <u>2</u> and a <u>GREEN</u> (2G) is <u>1 out of 9</u>, so   P(2G) = $\frac{1}{9}$.

7) If both spinners are <u>number spinners</u>, you can also
fill in the sample space with the <u>total of the two numbers</u>:

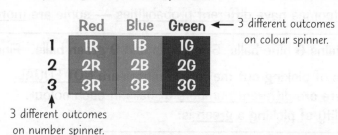

3 different outcomes on 2nd number spinner.

3 different outcomes on 1st number spinner.

	1	2	3
1	2	3	4
2	3	4	5
3	4	5	6

These are the totals of the two spinners, e.g. 3 + 3 = 6.

<u>Understanding probability — the outcome of learning this page...</u>

A sample space is a really handy way of making sure you've not missed out any possible outcomes.
1) Draw a sample space for rolling two dice together (both numbered 1-6), and answer these questions:
a) How many outcomes are there in total?   b) How many of the outcomes result in a total of 8?
c) What is the probability of rolling a total of 8 on the dice, P(8)?

Types of Data

Data is a fancy word for <u>information</u>. There are <u>different types</u> of data, which also have fancy names...

Data Can Be <u>Primary</u> Or <u>Secondary</u>

<u>PRIMARY</u> data is data <u>YOU'VE</u> collected.

There are <u>two</u> main ways you can get <u>primary data</u>:

- A <u>SURVEY</u>, e.g. a <u>questionnaire</u>.

- An <u>EXPERIMENT</u> (like you do in science lessons).

<u>SECONDARY</u> data is collected by <u>SOMEONE ELSE</u>.

There are lots of ways you can get <u>secondary data</u>, e.g. from:

- <u>newspapers</u>
- the <u>internet</u>
- <u>databases</u>
- <u>historical records</u>

Data can be <u>Qualitative</u> Or <u>Quantitative</u>

> Think 'quantity means numbers' as a way to remember which is which.

<u>QUALITATIVE</u> data is in <u>WORD</u> form.

For example:
- <u>gender</u> (male or female)
- eye <u>colour</u>
- <u>favourite</u> football team

<u>QUANTITATIVE</u> data is in <u>NUMBER</u> form.

For example:
- <u>heights</u> of people
- the <u>time taken</u> to do a task
- the <u>weight</u> of objects

<u>Quantitative</u> Data is <u>Discrete</u> or <u>Continuous</u>

<u>DISCRETE DATA</u> can be measured <u>exactly</u> — in <u>whole numbers</u> or <u>certain values</u>.

For example:
- the <u>number of goals</u> scored
- the <u>number of people</u> in a shop
- the <u>number of pages</u> in this book

<u>CONTINUOUS DATA</u> can take <u>any value</u> over a certain range.

For example:
- the <u>height</u> of <u>this page</u> (it's 297 mm <u>to the nearest mm</u> but that's not its <u>exact</u> height)
- the <u>weight</u> of a pumpkin
- the <u>length</u> of a carrot

Sorry, I can't date 'er — she's just not my type...

Just lots of <u>words</u> to learn on this page then. Once you've got that done, try this question:

Say whether this data is <u>qualitative</u>, <u>discrete</u> or <u>continuous</u>:

a) The number of people at a rugby match.

b) The colours of pebbles on a beach.

c) The names of people visiting a park on a certain day.

d) The lengths of fish in a pond.

Samples and Groups

Whatever the <u>type</u> of data, we have to <u>collect it</u> somehow. And there's <u>so much data</u> out there that to make things <u>simpler</u> we can take <u>samples</u>, and put things into <u>groups</u>.

Sampling — Cheaper and Easier than Asking Everyone

A sample is just part of the population.

1) We usually collect information about a <u>group of people or things</u>. This <u>whole group</u> is called a <u>POPULATION</u>.

   E.g. if you want to know the <u>heights of people in your school</u>, then the <u>population</u> is <u>everyone in the school</u>.

2) You can collect data by doing a <u>SURVEY</u> of either the <u>population</u> or a <u>SAMPLE</u>. A sample is just a <u>PART OF THE POPULATION</u>.

3) The sample has to <u>represent</u> the population <u>fairly</u> — this means that the <u>overall results</u> from the <u>sample</u> should be more or less <u>the same</u> as if they'd come from the <u>whole population</u>.

4) To <u>make sure</u> the sample represents the population fairly, it has to be <u>big enough</u>, chosen at <u>random</u>, and there must be the <u>right mix</u> of boys/girls, ages, etc. to <u>match the whole group</u>.

   If it doesn't represent the population fairly, it's a <u>biased</u> sample.

There are <u>pros and cons</u> of using samples:

PROS	CONS
It's a lot <u>quicker</u>, <u>cheaper</u> and often <u>easier</u> than asking the whole group.	You <u>don't</u> have results from <u>everyone</u> in the population so it can be <u>less accurate</u>.

Split Data Into Groups Called Classes

1) If there's a <u>lot of data</u>, or if it's very <u>spread out</u>, it's better to <u>group it</u> into different <u>classes</u>.

2) Choose the <u>classes</u> carefully so <u>none of them overlap</u>. Make sure each bit of data can <u>only</u> be put into <u>one class</u>.

3) For example, if you were collecting data on <u>ages</u>, it makes more sense to have <u>age groups</u> as shown below, instead of saying how many people were 15, how many were 16, etc.

Age in full years	0 – 19	20 – 39	40 – 59	60 – 79	80 – 99
Number of people	6	13	14	8	9

4) The <u>problem</u> with grouping data is that it's less <u>accurate</u> because you don't have the <u>individual values</u> any more. E.g. you can't tell how many people are <u>exactly 20 years old</u>.

"You said Clowns... and our survey said... 43... that's a top answer..."

If you <u>learn this stuff properly</u>, then maybe one day you too could work for a top game show...

Questionnaires

Questionnaires are a good way of collecting data — they're cheap and easy to give to lots of people.

Design Your Questionnaire Carefully

Most survey questions have a fixed number of answers, e.g. yes/no or tick box questions.
Think about the six points below when you get a question on questionnaires:

QUESTIONNAIRE ABOUT HOBBIES

1) How do you get to school? Please tick:

Bus ☐   Car ☐   Bicycle ☐

Walking ☐   Other ☐

1 QUESTIONS SHOULD BE RELEVANT
The question needs to be useful — this one has nothing to do with hobbies so it shouldn't be there.

2) What manner of recreational activities do you partake in to while away your leisure time?

2 QUESTIONS SHOULD BE CLEAR, SHORT AND EASY TO UNDERSTAND
This one isn't, so change it.

3) What is your favourite sport?

Football ☐   Hockey ☐

Baseball ☐   Tennis ☐

3 ALLOW FOR ALL POSSIBLE ANSWERS
This is hard to answer if you like rugby best. Add an 'other' box to allow for other answers.

4 QUESTIONS SHOULDN'T BE LEADING
Leading questions are ones that suggest what the answer should be. "What is your favourite hobby?" is a better question here.

4) Do you agree that knitting is the best hobby?   Yes /

5) Do you play computer games a lot?   Yes / No

6) How old are you?   ....

5 ANSWERS SHOULD BE CLEAR
It's not clear here what 'a lot' means. "How many hours do you play per week?" is better.

6 PEOPLE MAY NOT TELL THE TRUTH
They might be embarrassed about the answer. Here it'd be better to give an age group to choose from instead.

Question

Who wants to collect a questionnaire...

... is the (not so exciting) quiz spin-off. Make sure you learn this page and then try this question...
Give one thing that's wrong with each of these questions: a) Do you watch a lot of television?
b) Do you agree that maths is the most important school subject?
c) What is your favourite drink? Answer A, B or C.   A) Tea   B) Milk   C) Coffee

Mode, Median, Mean and Range

If you <u>learn the 3 types of average</u> (the mode, median and mean) — and what the <u>range</u> is — then you'll be well set for some juicy exam marks. But there's one thing you <u>must</u> remember...

THE GOLDEN RULE:

Always <u>WRITE THE NUMBERS</u> in <u>SIZE ORDER</u> first

We usually go from smallest to biggest.

E.g.   If you had a <u>list of shoe sizes</u> like this: 6, 7, 5, 5, 4, 9, 3
you'd need to write out the list <u>again</u> in <u>SIZE ORDER</u>, like <u>this</u>:   3, 4, 5, 5, 6, 7, 9

<u>There Are Three Types of Average</u>

1) <u>MODE</u> = <u>MOST</u> common

<u>Mode</u> = <u>mo</u>st (think of the 'o' when you say them)

2) <u>MEDIAN</u> = <u>MIDDLE</u> value

<u>Median</u> = <u>mid</u> (think of the <u>m*d</u> when you say them)

> **EXAMPLE:**
> In the list of <u>shoe sizes</u>:
>   3, 4, 5, <u>5</u>, 6, 7, 9
>
> The <u>mode</u> is '<u>5</u>' because it's the <u>most common</u> (it appears the most in the list).
>
> The <u>median</u> is also '<u>5</u>' because it's the <u>middle number</u>.

3) <u>MEAN</u> = <u>TOTAL</u> of items ÷ <u>NUMBER</u> of items

<u>Mean</u> is what most people think of when they say the <u>average</u>.
It's <u>mean</u> because you have to do a <u>calculation</u> to work it out.

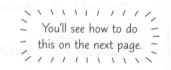

You'll see how to do this on the next page.

<u>Range <i>is How</i> Spread Out <i>Things Are</i></u>

<u>RANGE</u> = Biggest Number − Smallest Number

The <u>range</u> is <u>NOT</u> a type of <u>average</u>.
It's useful for seeing how <u>spread out</u> things are.
For example, in the list of shoe sizes above,
the <u>biggest</u> shoe size is <u>9</u> and the <u>smallest</u> is <u>3</u>.
So the <u>range</u> of shoe sizes = 9 − 3 = <u>6</u>.

<u>Don't forget the order — socks and then shoes...</u>

Learn the <u>four blue boxes</u> and the <u>Golden Rule</u>, then cover this page and write them all down.
Then you're ready for the next page — bet you can't wait...

Mode, Median, Mean and Range

Think you've got the last page sorted? <u>Good</u>. Let's have a look at another <u>example</u> then...

Example:

> Find the <u>MODE</u>, <u>MEDIAN</u>, <u>MEAN</u> and <u>RANGE</u> of these numbers:
>
> 2, 5, 3, 2, 6, -4, 0, 9, -3, 1, 6, 3, -2, 3

There are 14 numbers in the list so make a note of this.

<u>FIRST</u>... the <u>GOLDEN RULE</u>:

Write the numbers in <u>size order</u>:   -4, -3, -2, 0, 1, 2, 2, 3, 3, 3, 5, 6, 6, 9   (✓14)

Mode:

<u>MODE</u> = <u>most</u> common value, which is simply <u>3</u>.
This is because the number '3' <u>appears most in the list</u>.
(You can also say "The <u>modal</u> value is 3")

This bear is <u>NOT</u> smarter than the average bear.

Median:

<u>MEDIAN</u> = <u>the middle value</u> when they're <u>arranged in order of size</u>.

> -4, -3, -2, 0, 1, 2, 2, 3, 3, 3, 5, 6, 6, 9
> ← seven numbers this side ↑ seven numbers this side →

When there are <u>two middle numbers</u>, as in this case, then the
median is <u>halfway</u> between the <u>two middle numbers</u>.

To find the halfway point, <u>add them together</u> and <u>divide by 2</u>:   Median = (2 + 3) ÷ 2 = <u>2.5</u>.

Mean:

To find the <u>MEAN</u> — <u>add up all the numbers</u> in the list and <u>divide by how many there are</u>.

$$\text{MEAN} = \frac{\text{total}}{\text{number}} = \frac{-4 - 3 - 2 + 0 + 1 + 2 + 2 + 3 + 3 + 3 + 5 + 6 + 6 + 9}{14}$$

$$= 31 \div 14 = \underline{2.21}$$

Range:

<u>RANGE</u> = distance from lowest to highest value, i.e. from -4 up to 9 = <u>13</u>.

I don't mean to be mean — this stuff's important...

Use everything you've learnt on the last 2 pages to find the <u>mean</u>, <u>median</u>, <u>mode</u> and <u>range</u> for this list:
1, 3, 14, -5, 6, -12, 18, 7, 23, 10, -5, -14, 0, 25, 8

Frequency Tables

Frequency tables are like tally charts. They can either be done in rows or in columns of numbers. They're not too bad if you learn these key points:

> 1) The word FREQUENCY means HOW MANY.
>   So a frequency table is just a 'How many in each group' table.
>
> 2) The FIRST ROW (or column) gives the GROUP LABELS.
>
> 3) The FREQUENCY ROW (or column) tells you
>   HOW MANY THERE ARE in that group.

You can use frequency tables to help draw things like bar charts (p. 71) and pie charts (p. 72-73).

Example:

46 pupils in a school were asked how many sisters they had.
The results were put into a frequency table as shown:

In Columns:

No. of Sisters	Frequency
0	7
1	15
2	12
3	8
4	3
5	1
6	0
Total:	46

Group labels.

In Rows:

No. of Sisters	0	1	2	3	4	5	6	Total:
Tally	ℍℍ II	ℍℍ ℍℍ ℍℍ	ℍℍ ℍℍ II	ℍℍ III	III	I		
Frequency	7	15	12	8	3	1	0	46

The tally column is usually left out.

The frequency is just a total of the tally for that group.

You can use the table to find the averages and range:

1) The MODE is the group with the HIGHEST FREQUENCY.

   In this case most people asked said they had 1 sister, so the MODE is 1.

2) The table tells us there are people with anything from '0 sisters' right up to '5 sisters' (but NOT 6 sisters).

   So the RANGE is 5 − 0 = 5.

3) To find the MEAN you need to add an extra row to the table — see next page.

My table has 5 columns, 6 rows and 4 legs...

The best way of getting your head round this stuff is to practise doing it, so have a go yourself. You could ask your class how many times they've been to London, then put the results in a frequency table.

Finding The Mean From Frequency Tables

So you're feeling okay with <u>frequency tables</u> now? Good. One last thing to learn then.
Finding the <u>mean</u> may seem hard at first, but take your time and <u>learn the steps</u>...

You Need To Add An Extra Row

Let's look again at our <u>frequency table of sisters</u> from the last page:

No. of Sisters	0	1	2	3	4	5	6	Total:
Frequency	7	15	12	8	3	1	0	46

(People asked)

1) If we had a <u>list</u> of the number of sisters everyone had, it would look like <u>this</u>:

0, 0, 0, 0, 0, 0, 0, 1, 1, 1, 1, 1, 1, 1, 1, 1, 1, 1, 1, 1, 1, 1, 2, 2, 2, 2, 2, 2, 2, 2....

    7 lots of O   15 lots of 1

2) There would be <u>46 numbers</u> in the list because that's how many people were asked.

3) To find the <u>mean</u> from the <u>list</u> you would have to <u>add up all the numbers</u> and <u>divide by 46</u>.

4) It's <u>exactly the same</u> for the table — except we <u>cheat</u> by adding an <u>extra row</u>:

No. of Sisters	0	1	2	3	4	5	6	Total:
Frequency	7	15	12	8	3	1	0	46
No. × Frequency	0 × 7 = <u>0</u>	1 × 15 = <u>15</u>	2 × 12 = <u>24</u>	3 × 8 = <u>24</u>	4 × 3 = <u>12</u>	5 × 1 = <u>5</u>	6 × 0 = <u>0</u>	0 + 15 + 24 + 24 + 12 + 5 + 0 = <u>80</u>

¯ This is the same as ¯
¯ adding 7 lots of O. ¯

¯ This is the same as ¯
¯ adding 3 lots of 4. ¯

¯ This is the same as adding up all ¯
the numbers in the list.
¯ It's the <u>total number of sisters</u>. ¯

5) Now from the <u>table</u>:

> <u>MEAN</u> = 3rd Row Total ÷ 2nd Row Total
> = 80 ÷ 46 = <u>1.74</u> (sisters per person)

Hahahaa!

Mean sisters

Always Follow These Steps...

1) Add up the <u>TOTAL</u> of the <u>SECOND ROW</u> (or column).

2) Make a <u>THIRD ROW</u> (or column) by <u>MULTIPLYING</u> the <u>FIRST ROW</u> and <u>SECOND ROW</u> together.

3) Add up the <u>TOTAL</u> of the new <u>THIRD ROW</u>.

4)
> <u>MEAN</u> = 3rd Row total ÷ 2nd Row Total

Do you know what I mean...?

I'm not going to lie and say that was an easy page, but it's really not as bad as it looks. The trick is to <u>learn the 4 steps</u> in the red box and do it <u>every time</u> you're asked for the mean from a table.

Line Graphs and Pictograms

Data can be shown in different types of <u>charts</u>, <u>tables</u> and <u>graphs</u>. <u>Line graphs</u> and <u>pictograms</u> make it <u>easier to see</u> what the data <u>shows</u> than if it was just written in a list or a table.

Line Graphs

1) A <u>line graph</u> is a set of points joined with straight lines.

2) They often have '<u>time</u>' along the bottom to show how something is <u>changing</u> over time:

3) You can draw <u>two line graphs</u> on the same grid to <u>compare</u> the two, as shown below.

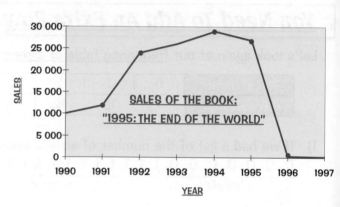

These graphs show clearly that as the year went on, <u>fewer</u> people wore <u>earmuffs</u> and <u>more</u> people wore <u>bikinis</u>...

Pictograms

1) PICTOGRAMS use <u>pictures</u> in place of <u>numbers</u> to show frequency.

2) In a pictogram each <u>picture</u> or <u>symbol</u> represents a <u>certain number of items</u>.

EXAMPLE:

The <u>pictogram</u> below shows the <u>number of talking cats</u> used in TV adverts over <u>3 months</u>:

🐱 = 500 talking cats

May	🐱 🐱 🐱	(3 × 500 = <u>1500</u> talking cats)
June	🐱 🐱 🐱	(2.5 × 500 = <u>1250</u> talking cats)
July	🐱 🐱 🐱 🐱	(4 × 500 = <u>2000</u> talking cats)

Total = 1500 + 1250 + 2000 = <u>4750</u> ridiculous talking cats.

A picture paints a thousand words...

🐱 = learn the page, cover it up, and see what you can remember. 🐱🐱🐱🐱🐱🐱🐱🐱🐱...

Two-Way Tables

Two-way tables are a bit like frequency tables but they show two different things at the same time. Like eye colour and hair colour. Or your favourite type of jelly and whether you like mushrooms...

Example:

"Use this table to work out how many

(a) right-handed people and

(b) left-handed women

there were in this survey."

This means that 27 out of the 400 people asked were left-handed men.

	Women	Men	TOTAL
Left-handed		27	63
Right-handed	164	173	
TOTAL	200	200	400

Total left-handed + Total right-handed = Total no. of people

Total no. of women + Total no. of men = Total no. of people

Answer:

(a) To find the number of right-handed people, EITHER:

(i) Add up the number of right-handed women and the number of right-handed men.
So that's 164 + 173 = 337 right-handed people.

OR:

(ii) Take away the total number of left-handed people from the total number of people.
So that's 400 – 63 = 337 right-handed people.

	Women	Men	TOTAL
Left-handed		27	63
Right-handed	164	173	
TOTAL	200	200	400

(b) To find the number of left-handed women, EITHER:

(i) Take away the number of right-handed women from the total number of women.
That's 200 – 164 = 36 left-handed women.

OR:

(ii) Take away the left-handed men from the total number of left-handed people.
Which would be 63 – 27 = 36 left-handed women.

	Women	Men	TOTAL
Left-handed		27	63
Right-handed	164	173	
TOTAL	200	200	400

There's no two ways about it — you've got to learn it...

Try filling out a similar table for the people in your class. Count how many girls are left- or right-handed, and the same for the boys, and add up the totals of the rows and columns. Fun times.

Scatter Graphs

Scatter Graphs Can Show Correlation

1) A SCATTER GRAPH is used to show how two things are related (linked).

2) If they're closely related then the points will lie fairly close to a straight line,
called a LINE OF BEST FIT.
You say the data has STRONG CORRELATION.

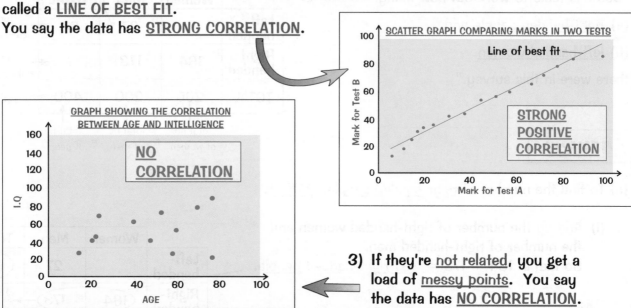

3) If they're not related, you get a
load of messy points. You say
the data has NO CORRELATION.

4) If the points form a line sloping UPHILL from left to right (like the first graph above),
then there is POSITIVE CORRELATION — both things increase or decrease together.

5) If the points form a line sloping DOWNHILL from left to right (like the graph below),
then there is NEGATIVE CORRELATION — as one thing increases the other decreases.

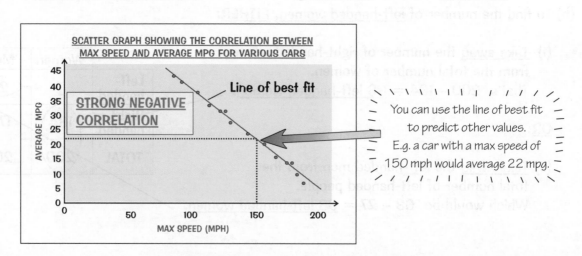

You can use the line of best fit
to predict other values.
E.g. a car with a max speed of
150 mph would average 22 mpg.

What soap do maths teachers watch — Correlation Street...

There is a strong positive correlation between evil laughing/cat stroking/beard combing and how much of
an evil genius you are. Learn this page and try drawing an example of each type of scatter graph.

Bar Charts

Bar Charts *Show Data As Bars*

1) The <u>height</u> of each bar is the <u>frequency</u> for that group.

2) Watch out for when the bars should <u>touch</u> or <u>not touch</u>:

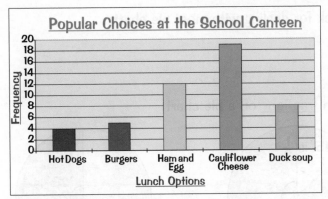

Popular Choices at the School Canteen

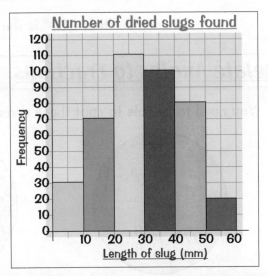

Number of dried slugs found

This bar chart compares <u>separate items</u>
(e.g. hot dogs, burgers) so the bars <u>don't touch</u>.

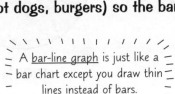

A <u>bar-line graph</u> is just like a
bar chart except you draw thin
lines instead of bars.

<u>ALL</u> the bars in this chart are for <u>LENGTHS</u> —
<u>every possible length</u> must be included so there
should be <u>no spaces</u> between the bars.

Dual Bar Charts *Can be Used to Compare Things*

1) <u>Dual</u> bar charts show <u>two</u> sets of data
together so you can <u>compare them</u>.

2) Each category has <u>two bars</u>
— <u>one for each set of data</u>.

3) The dual bar chart on the right shows the
favourite colours of a group of pupils, but
it's split into two sets — <u>boys</u> and <u>girls</u>.

4) The bar chart shows, for example, that
<u>green</u> was the <u>most popular colour</u> for
girls, but <u>red</u> was the favourite for boys.

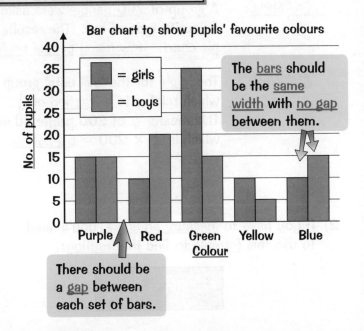

Bar chart to show pupils' favourite colours

The <u>bars</u> should
be the <u>same</u>
<u>width</u> with <u>no gap</u>
between them.

There should be
a <u>gap</u> between
each set of bars.

A sheep's favourite graph — the baaaa chart...

Woah, have another read of this page, then test yourself with this lovely question.

Use this table to draw a <u>dual bar chart</u> showing
how the four teams scored in each round of a quiz.

Hint: Each colour team should have two bars — one for each round.

Team Name	Green	Blue	Red	Yellow
Points — 1st round	24	15	20	25
Points — 2nd round	16	15	22	20

Pie Charts

Just as you can make a yummy pie from the right mix of meat and pastry, examiners can make meaty exam questions from <u>pie charts</u>. So learn the <u>GOLDEN RULE</u> for pie charts:

The TOTAL of Everything = 360°

Remember that 360° is the trick for dealing with most pie charts.

Relate Angles to Fractions

1) You need to be able to spot these common <u>fractions</u> on a pie chart:

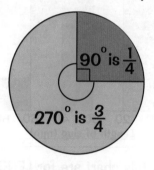 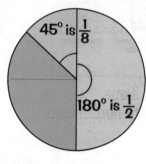 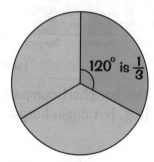

$90°$ is $\frac{1}{4}$
$270°$ is $\frac{3}{4}$

$45°$ is $\frac{1}{8}$
$180°$ is $\frac{1}{2}$

$120°$ is $\frac{1}{3}$

<u>EXAMPLE:</u> A group of <u>200 people</u> were asked to choose their favourite type of cat. The results are shown in this pie chart. <u>How many people prefer evil cats?</u>

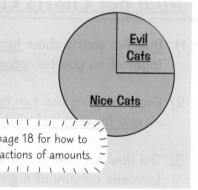

<u>ANSWER:</u> The <u>angle</u> for the 'evil cats' group is <u>90°</u>, which relates to a <u>fraction</u> of $\frac{1}{4}$. This means $\frac{1}{4}$ of 200 preferred evil cats, which is $\frac{1}{4} \times 200 = \underline{50\ people}$.

See page 18 for how to find fractions of amounts.

2) If you have to <u>measure an angle</u>, you'll need to use this <u>formula</u> to find the <u>fraction</u>:

$$\text{Fraction} = \frac{\text{Angle}}{360°}$$

Have a look at page 47 if you're not sure how to measure an angle.

3) For example, if the angle for a group is <u>36°</u>, the <u>fraction</u> is $36 \div 360 = \frac{1}{10}$. So the <u>number</u> of things in that group will be $\frac{1}{10}$ of the <u>total</u>.

Pie Charts

Work Out Angles to Draw Pie Charts

<u>EXAMPLE:</u>   The table below shows the results of a survey on the <u>animals people are most afraid of</u>.
<u>Draw a pie chart</u> to show these results.

Creature	Hamsters	Guinea pigs	Rabbits	Ducks	Stick insects	Total
Number	20	17	15	26	12	90 ①
Angle	80°					360° ②

③ ↓ ×4   ×4

1) Add up all the numbers in each sector to get the <u>TOTAL</u> (=90).

2) Then find the number that you need to times the
<u>total</u> by to get <u>360°</u>. 360 ÷ 90 = 4, so the total needs to
be multiplied by 4 to make 360°.

3) Now <u>MULTIPLY EVERY NUMBER BY 4</u> to get the
angle for each group. E.g. the angle for hamsters
is 20 × 4 = <u>80°</u>.

4) Draw a '<u>start line</u>' somewhere in the circle and draw the <u>angle</u>
of one group from this line. Use <u>this</u> angle line as the start line
for the <u>next angle</u>, and <u>carry on</u> until all the angles are done.

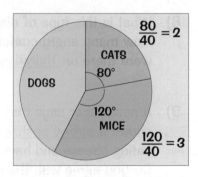

Start Line

12 Stick
Insects
48°

20
Hamsters
80°   ④

26 Ducks
104°

17
Guinea
Pigs
60° 68°

15
Rabbits

There should be no gaps
if you've drawn all the
angles right.

Use the Total to Find the Other Numbers

<u>EXAMPLE:</u>   In the pie chart on the right, there are <u>9 pets in total</u>.
How many <u>dogs</u> are there?

<u>ANSWER:</u>

1) <u>Divide</u> 360° by the <u>total number of pets</u>: 360° ÷ 9 = 40°.
40° represents <u>one pet</u>.

2) Divide <u>each of the angles given</u> by 40° to get the number of pets
for those groups. So there are 2 cats and 3 mice, as shown.

3) The final bit of pie is what's <u>left over</u>: 9 – 2 – 3 = 4 pet dogs.

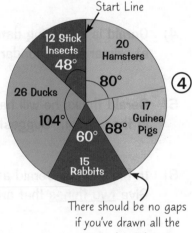

$\frac{80}{40} = 2$

CATS
80°

DOGS

120°
MICE

$\frac{120}{40} = 3$

I bet you were expecting a joke about pies here...

... I'm far too witty to bother making jokes about pies on a page about pie charts. There's just no need
to go on about tasty steak-filled pies on a bed of creamy mash and a side order of mushy peas... mmm.

Anyway, while I'm off eating pies,
you can <u>draw a pie chart</u> for this table:

Football Team	Wigan A.	Luton	Man Utd	Others
No. of fans	53	15	30	22

Revision Test for Section Five

1) The probability of rolling <u>SIX</u> on a biased dice is <u>0.2</u>.
   What is the chance of <u>NOT</u> rolling a six?

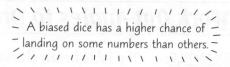

A biased dice has a higher chance of landing on some numbers than others.

2) Colin has made a game for the summer fair. In a bag he has <u>3 red balls</u>,
   <u>5 green balls</u> and <u>7 black balls</u>. If you pick a red ball you win a prize.
   What is the <u>probability</u> of winning Colin's game, as a <u>percentage</u>?

3) I toss a coin and throw a dice at the same time.
   a) <u>List all the possible outcomes</u> in a <u>sample space</u>.
   b) What is the probability of getting <u>a HEAD and a SIX</u>?

4) Gerald is collecting data <u>for himself</u> about <u>shoe sizes</u> of people in his school. Is this data:
   a) primary or secondary?   b) qualitative or quantitative?   c) discrete or continuous?

5) Gerald thinks he will have <u>too much information</u> if he writes down the shoe size of every person
   in the school. Suggest <u>two things</u> that would make it <u>easier</u> to collect the data.

6) In his survey, Gerald asks the question: "<u>Do you have big feet?</u>".
   Give <u>two things</u> that are wrong with this question.

7) For this set of numbers:

   2, 6, 7, 12, 3, 7, 4, 15

   a) Find the <u>MODE</u>   b) Find the <u>MEDIAN</u>
   c) Find the <u>MEAN</u>   d) Find the <u>RANGE</u>

8) What is this type of diagram called?
   How many angry customers
   were there on <u>Thursday</u>?

9) A newspaper says that the scatter graph shown here
   shows a <u>strong positive correlation</u> between
   eating cheese and having nightmares.
   Do you agree with the newspaper?

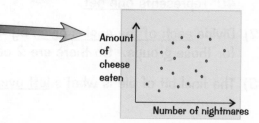

10) Fiona has done a traffic survey for her Geography coursework.
    She wants to show the information in a pie chart.
    a) <u>Complete Fiona's table</u>.
    b) Draw the <u>PIE CHART</u>.

Car Colour	Blue	Red	Yellow	White	Totals:
Number of Cars	12	15	4	9	40
Angle on Pie Chart					360°

X and Y Coordinates

Graph questions can be fun. OK, maybe not fun, but better than being out in a hail storm in just your pants. First, you need to know the basics...

Plot Coordinates On a Grid

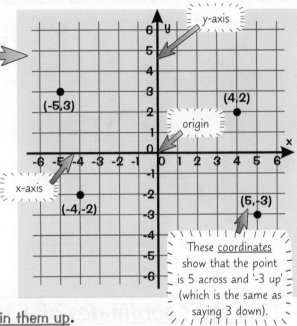

1) You draw graphs on a grid, a bit like this one.

2) It's made by two lines crossing — called the axes.

3) The y-axis goes from bottom to top, and the x-axis goes from left to right.

4) They meet at the point with coordinates (0, 0) — this is called the origin.

5) Coordinates are a pair of numbers that tell us where a point is on the grid.

6) The x-coordinate tells us how far along, and the y-coordinate tells us how far up to draw a point.

7) To plot (draw) a graph, plot coordinates first then join them up.

These coordinates show that the point is 5 across and '-3 up' (which is the same as saying 3 down).

X, Y Coordinates — Getting them in the Right Order

1) You must always give coordinates in brackets like this: (x, y)

2) And you always have to be real careful to get them the right way round, x first, then y.

3) Here are three ways you could remember:

$$(x , y)$$

1) The two coordinates are always in ALPHABETICAL ORDER, x then y.

2) x is always the flat axis going ACROSS the page.
   In other words 'x is a...cross'   Get it — x is a 'x'. (Hilarious isn't it.)

3) Remember it's always IN THE HOUSE (→) and then UP THE STAIRS (↑)
   so it's ALONG first and then UP, i.e. x-coordinate first, and then y-coordinate.

But what if you live in a bungalow?...

In that case, you just have to imagine where the stairs would be.
So, make sure you learn one of the 3 Rules for getting x and y the right way round. Then turn over and see what you can remember.

1) Write down the coordinates of the letters A to H on this graph:

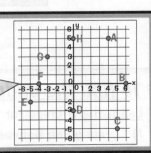

Midpoint of a Line Segment

When you get down to it, finding the midpoint is just <u>adding</u> and then <u>dividing by two</u>. Hurrah.

The 'Midpoint' is just the Middle of the Line

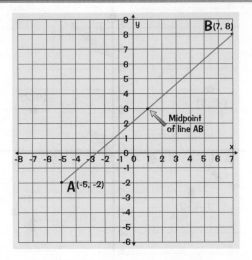

The '<u>MIDPOINT OF A LINE SEGMENT</u>' is the <u>POINT THAT'S BANG IN THE MIDDLE</u> of it.

Midpoint of Jeff

Find the Coordinates of a Midpoint

1) You need to know how to find the <u>coordinates of a midpoint</u>.

2) For a line drawn between <u>two points</u>, find the <u>average</u> of the <u>two x-coordinates</u>, and the <u>average</u> of the <u>two y-coordinates</u>.

3) These two <u>averages</u> are the <u>coordinates of the midpoint</u>.

> To find the average of two numbers, add them together and divide by 2.

<u>EXAMPLE</u>: A and B have coordinates (2, 1) and (6, 3). Find the <u>midpoint of the line AB</u>.

START BY SKETCHING A GRAPH

Then follow these <u>THREE STEPS</u>...

1) Find the <u>average</u> of the <u>x-coordinates</u> of the two points.	Average of x-coordinates = (2 + 6) ÷ 2 = <u>4</u>
2) Find the <u>average</u> of the <u>y-coordinates</u> of the two points.	Average of y-coordinates = (1 + 3) ÷ 2 = <u>2</u>
3) Put them in <u>brackets</u>.	Put them in brackets (x-coordinate first): (<u>4</u>, <u>2</u>)

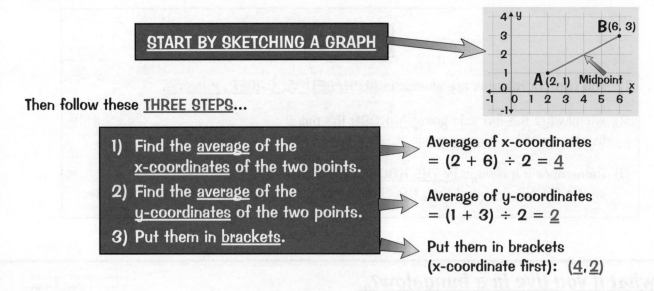

To find the midpoint — average, average, brackets...

<u>Learn the 3 steps</u> for finding midpoints. Then plot these points on some graph paper: A(1, 4), B(5, 6).

1) Draw a line between points A and B and find the midpoint of the line AB.

Straight-Line Graphs

If you thought I-spy was fun, wait until you play 'spot the graph from its equation'.

Horizontal and Vertical Lines: E.g. x = 3 and y = –2

Vertical lines are always "x = a number"

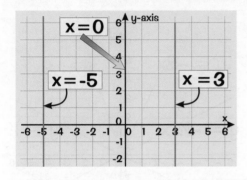

x=0

x=-5

x=3

1) E.g. <u>x = -5</u> is a <u>vertical line through '-5'</u> on the x-axis.

2) The <u>y-axis</u> is also the line <u>x = 0</u>.

Horizontal lines are always "y = a number"

1) E.g. <u>y = 3</u> is a <u>horizontal line through '3'</u> on the y-axis.

2) The <u>x-axis</u> is also the line <u>y = 0</u>.

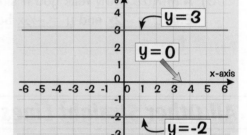

y=3

y=0

y=-2

The Main Diagonals: "y = x" and "y = –x"

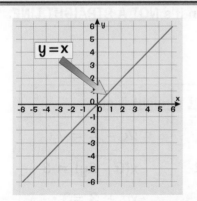

y=x

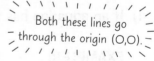
Both these lines go through the origin (O,O).

'<u>y = x</u>' is the <u>main diagonal</u> that goes <u>UPHILL</u> from left to right.

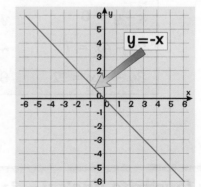

y=-x

'<u>y = -x</u>' is the <u>main diagonal</u> that goes <u>DOWNHILL</u> from left to right.

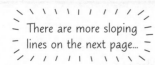
There are more sloping lines on the next page...

Straight-Line Graphs

Joy of joys, here are <u>more graphs</u> to learn...

Other <u>Sloping Lines</u> Through the Origin: <u>"y = ax" and "y = –ax"</u>

<u>y = ax</u> and <u>y = –ax</u> are equations for
<u>SLOPING LINES THROUGH THE ORIGIN</u>
(where 'a' is <u>just a number</u>).

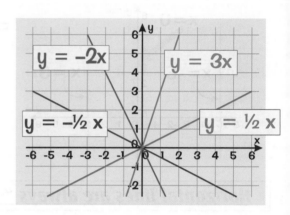

1) The value of '<u>a</u>' (known as the <u>gradient</u>)
tells you the <u>steepness</u> of the line.

2) The <u>bigger</u> 'a' is, the <u>steeper</u> the slope.
E.g. the line <u>y = 3x</u> on the right is <u>steeper</u> than
<u>y = ½x</u>, because <u>3 is bigger than ½</u>.

3) A <u>MINUS SIGN</u> tells you it slopes <u>DOWNHILL</u>.
E.g. <u>y = –2x</u> and <u>y = –½x</u> both slope <u>downhill</u>.

All Other <u>Straight Lines</u>

1) Other straight-line equations are a little more tricky.

2) The next page shows you how to <u>draw them</u>,
but the first step is <u>spotting them</u> in the first place.

It doesn't have to have <u>all</u> of these
bits (e.g. x = 2 is still a straight
line) but straight lines won't have
<u>anything other</u> than these bits.

3) <u>STRAIGHT-LINE EQUATIONS</u> just have '<u>SOMETHING X, SOMETHING Y, AND A NUMBER</u>'.

4) If an equation has things like x^2 (or other <u>powers</u>), xy or $\frac{1}{x}$, then it's <u>NOT A STRAIGHT LINE</u>.

<u>EXAMPLES</u>:

<u>Straight lines:</u>	
$x - y = 0$	$y = 2 + 3x$
$2y - 4x = 7$	$4x - 3 = 5y$
$3y + 3x = 12$	$6y - x - 7 = 0$

<u>NOT straight lines:</u>	
$y = x^3 + 3$	$2y - \frac{1}{x} = 7$
$\frac{1}{y} + \frac{1}{x} = 2$	$x(3 - 2y) = 3$
$x^2 = 4 - y$	$xy + 3 = 0$

<u>My favourite line's y = 3x, it gets the chicks every time...</u>

OK, maybe not every time, but it's still worth learning all this stuff.
When you think you know it, turn over the page and see what you can remember.

Straight-Line Graphs

Strap on a beret, grab a pencil and let's get arty (well, graphy at least) — it's <u>graph drawing</u> time.
In the exam, you'll probably get a <u>table</u> to fill in, and be asked to plot a <u>graph</u> from an <u>equation</u>.

> **EXAMPLE:** Complete this <u>table of values</u>
> using the equation <u>y = 2x – 7</u>,
> and use it to <u>plot a graph</u> of y = 2x – 7.

x	-2	0	2	4	6
y	-11		-3		

1) Doing the Table of Values

1) Put <u>each x-value</u> into the equation and work out the <u>matching y-values</u>.
2) E.g. <u>for x = 0</u>, y = 2x – 7 = (2 × 0) – 7 = 0 – 7 = <u>-7</u> ...
3) ...and <u>for x = 4</u>, y = 2x – 7 = (2 × 4) – 7 = 8 – 7 = <u>1</u> etc. until you get:

x	-2	0	2	4	6
y	-11	-7	-3	1	5

2) Plotting The Points and Drawing The Graph

1) <u>PLOT EACH PAIR</u> of x- and y-values <u>CAREFULLY</u> from the table as a point on the graph.
2) The points will form <u>A DEAD STRAIGHT LINE</u>.
3) Draw a line <u>through them</u> with a <u>RULER</u>.

x	-2	0	2	4	6
y	-11	-7	-3	1	5
(x,y)	(-2,-11)	(0,-7)	(2,-3)	(4,1)	(6,5)

These are the <u>coordinates</u> you need to plot.
Look back at page 75 if you need to.

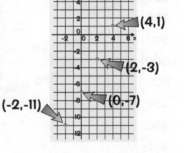

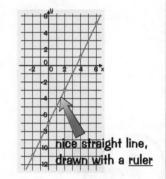

nice straight line,
drawn with a ruler

4) <u>NEVER</u> let one point stick out from the rest.
You should <u>never get SPIKES</u> on a straight-line graph.

5) If one point does look a <u>bit odd</u>, check 2 things:
   a) the <u>y-value</u> you worked out in the <u>table</u>
   b) that you've <u>plotted it properly</u>.

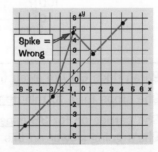

Spike = Wrong

Careful plotting — the key to perfect graphs and being an evil genius...

... mwah ha ha ha. Learn this page, then have a go at the questions below.

1) <u>Complete this table of values</u> for the equation: y = x – 2
2) Then <u>plot the points on graph paper and draw the graph.</u>

x	-4	-2	-1	0	1	2	4
y	-6			-2			

Travel Graphs

Yay, just what you wanted to see — some <u>more graphs</u>...

Know What Travel Graphs Show

> 1) A <u>TRAVEL GRAPH</u> shows <u>DISTANCE</u> (↑) against <u>TIME</u> (→) for a <u>MOVING OBJECT</u> (e.g. a car, person, goat...).
> 2) <u>FLAT SECTIONS</u> show where the object has <u>STOPPED</u>.
> 3) The <u>STEEPER</u> the graph the <u>FASTER</u> it's going.
> 4) The graph <u>GOING UP</u> means it's travelling <u>AWAY</u>.
> 5) The graph <u>COMING DOWN</u> means it's <u>COMING BACK AGAIN</u>.

Example: Travel Graph For A Cyclist...

> **EXAMPLE:** The <u>travel graph below</u> shows the journey of Sarah, out on a bike ride. Explain what's happening at <u>each stage</u> of Sarah's journey.

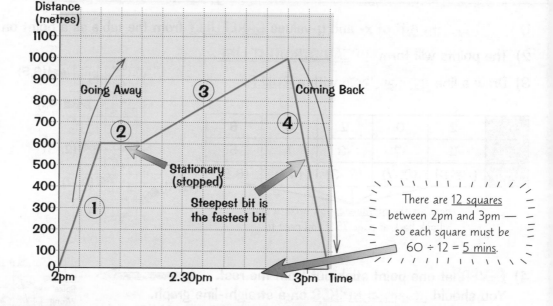

There are <u>12 squares</u> between 2pm and 3pm — so each square must be 60 ÷ 12 = <u>5 mins</u>.

1) Sarah rides <u>600 m away</u> from her house at a <u>steady speed</u> for <u>10 mins</u>.
2) She <u>stops</u> for a <u>10 minute rest</u> (<u>flat</u> means 'stopped')
3) She <u>carries on</u> for <u>35 mins</u>, doing another <u>400 m</u> — she's now <u>1000 m</u> from her house. She's going <u>slower</u> on this bit — you can tell because the graph <u>isn't as steep</u>.
4) In this last bit, Sarah rides the full <u>1000 m back to her house</u> in one go, in <u>10 mins</u>. She's going <u>fastest</u> on this bit — you can tell because the graph is <u>steepest</u> here.

Learning maths is just like riding a bike...

...except without the grazed knees when you fall off. The trick is — once you've <u>learnt it</u>, you'll find it a lot easier to <u>remember</u> how to do it <u>again</u>, in the exam say. So <u>start pedalling</u> and <u>learn this page</u>...

Conversion Graphs

In the exam you might get a question with a <u>conversion graph</u> which helps you switch between different <u>units</u> — for things like <u>money</u> (£ → Dollars) or <u>speed</u> (mph → km/h) etc.

Know How to Read Off Conversion Graphs

1) <u>Draw a line</u> from the <u>VALUE YOU KNOW</u> on one axis.

2) Keep going until you <u>hit the LINE</u>.

3) Then <u>CHANGE DIRECTION</u> and go straight to <u>the other axis</u>.

4) <u>READ OFF THE NEW VALUE</u> from the axis. <u>That's the answer.</u>

Example: Conversion Graph For Distances

This graph converts between <u>miles</u> and <u>kilometres</u>:

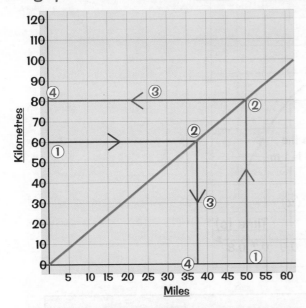

EXAMPLE 1: How many miles is 60 km?

<u>ANSWER:</u>

1) Draw a line <u>straight across</u> from '60' on the 'km' axis...

2) ...until it <u>hits the line</u>...

3) ...then go <u>straight down</u> to the 'miles' axis...

4) ...and read off the answer: <u>37.5 miles</u>

EXAMPLE 2: How many km is 50 miles?

<u>ANSWER:</u>

1) Draw a line <u>straight up</u> from '50' on the 'miles' axis...

2) ...until it <u>hits the line</u>...

3) ...then go <u>straight across</u> to the 'km' axis...

4) ...and read off the answer: <u>80 km</u>

Convert this page into exam marks...

You might hear about "<u>ready reckoner</u>" graphs — these are just <u>conversion graphs</u> that make it easy to do <u>calculations</u>, so treat them just the same. You'll need to <u>learn this page</u> first though.

Reading Off Graphs

It doesn't matter what <u>type</u> of graph you get — distance and time, chickens and aliens — to <u>read values</u> from a graph you just need to follow the same method every time.

Getting Answers From Your Graph

> FOR A SINGLE CURVE OR LINE, you <u>ALWAYS</u> get the answer by:
> 1) <u>drawing a straight line to the graph from one axis</u>,
> 2) and then <u>down or across to the other axis</u>.

Example:

The graph shows the <u>height of a ball</u> as it is thrown through the air.
<u>Use the graph</u> to find the approximate <u>times</u> when the ball was <u>1 m above the ground</u>.

<u>Approximate</u> just means you don't have to be exact, just give roughly the right answer.

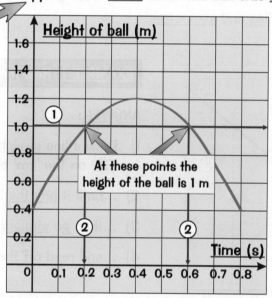

At these points the height of the ball is 1 m

METHOD:

1) Draw a <u>straight line across</u> the graph at <u>1.0</u> on the <u>vertical</u> ↑ axis ('height of ball') — this is where the height of the ball is <u>1 m</u>.

2) This line crosses the graph <u>twice</u>.
Draw <u>straight lines down</u> to the <u>horizontal</u> → axis ('time') at these points and <u>read off</u> the values:

Time = <u>0.2 s</u> and <u>0.6 s</u>.

ANSWER: So the ball was <u>1 m</u> above the ground at <u>0.2 s</u> and <u>0.6 s</u>.

Right graph — we're not leaving here 'til I get some answers...

<u>Learn</u> the <u>rules for getting answers from your graph</u>. Then turn over... you know what to do by now...

Revision Test for Section Six

1) Claire and James are playing <u>battleships</u>.
   Their grids, with their ships shown in grey, are drawn below.
   a) Claire guesses the point (7, 2) on James's grid. Has she hit a ship?
   b) James guesses (4, 6) on Claire's grid. Has he hit a ship?

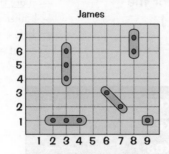

James

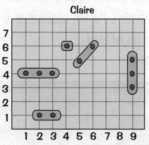

Claire

2) Plot these <u>points</u> on a grid: A(0,4), B(-4,2), C(-3,-5), D(5,-6), E(5,0).
   Copy the grid from page 75 if you need to.

3) On the grid you've just drawn for question 2),
   join point A to point B and find the <u>midpoint</u> of AB.

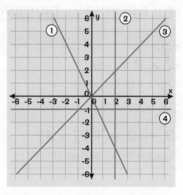

4) Look at the grid to the right.
   Which line has the <u>equation</u>:
   a) x = 2,
   b) y = -1,
   c) y = x,
   d) y = -2x?

5) a) Complete the <u>table of values</u> below for the equation: y = x + 3
   b) <u>Draw the graph</u>.

x	-5	-3	-1	0	1	2	4	6
y	-2				4			

6) The <u>travel graph</u> on the right shows the
   journey of a goat walking along a road.
   Describe what the goat is doing:
   a) Between <u>4 pm and 6 pm</u>.
   b) Between <u>6 pm and 7 pm</u>.
   c) How <u>far from home</u> does the goat stray?

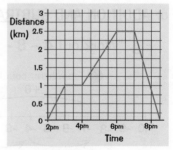

7) At the market, Farmer Miles can trade in his sheep for chickens, or trade in chickens
   for sheep. The <u>conversion graph</u> below helps him find what the animals are worth.
   a) How many sheep can he get for <u>15 chickens</u>?
   b) How many chickens can he get for <u>10 sheep</u>?

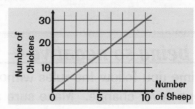

Negative Numbers

Negative numbers are just numbers <u>less than zero</u>. You might come across them on a freezing day, when the <u>temperature</u> drops. Or possibly on your bank statement if you've spent too much...

Rules *For* Multiplying *and* Dividing

1) When doing calculations you have to watch out for the <u>signs</u> of the numbers: <u>positive</u> (+) or <u>negative</u> (−).

2) The signs in the <u>question</u> can affect the <u>sign of the answer</u>, like so:

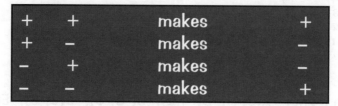

Positive numbers are numbers <u>more than zero</u>. We don't usually bother putting the positive sign (+) before them, so if a number hasn't got a sign, it must be <u>positive</u>.

+	+	makes	+
+	−	makes	−
−	+	makes	−
−	−	makes	+

3) <u>BUT</u> this <u>ONLY</u> works in the following <u>TWO CASES</u>:

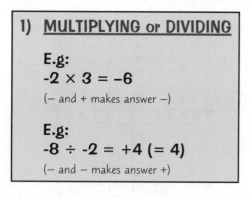

1) MULTIPLYING or DIVIDING

E.g:
-2 × 3 = −6
(− and + makes answer −)

E.g:
-8 ÷ -2 = +4 (= 4)
(− and − makes answer +)

2) When two signs appear NEXT TO each other

Two − signs together can be changed to one + sign.

E.g:
5 − -4 = 5 + 4 = 9

− and − together changed to one +.

E.g:
4 + -6 − -7 = 4 − 6 + 7 = 5

+ and − together changed to one −.

These aren't next to each other so don't combine them.

Use *a* Number Line *To* Add *Or* Subtract

For <u>ADDITION AND SUBTRACTION</u> with negative numbers, use a <u>NUMBER LINE</u>:

E.g. "Work out 4 − 8 − 3 + 6"

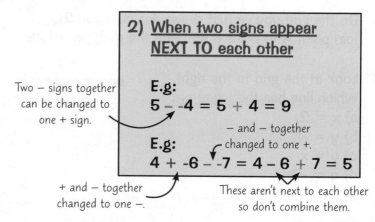

Ⓒ From here, count <u>6 up</u>.
+6

Ⓓ Finish at -1, so this is the answer.

-10 -9 -8 -7 -6 -5 -4 -3 -2 -1 0 1 2 3 4 5 6 7 8 9 10

−3

−8

Ⓑ From here, count another <u>3 down</u>.

Ⓐ <u>Start at 4</u> and count <u>8 down</u>.

So 4 − 8 − 3 + 6 = <u>-1</u>

Good evening caller, you're through to the Number Line. What's your problem?

Now stop being so negative — this stuff's not so bad...

Most of the time you follow the rules without thinking — because we <u>usually</u> work with <u>positive numbers</u> where the signs never change. Make sure you've <u>learnt everything on the page</u>, then try these:

1) Work out   a) -4 × -3   b) -4 + -5 + 3   c) 12 ÷ -4   d) (3 + -2 − 4) ÷ (2 + -5)

Powers and Letters

Right. __LEARN THIS PAGE__, then __PEEL ME SOME GRAPES__ and __IRON MY SHIRTS__.
Sorry, I think the power's gone to my head...

Powers Make Things Look Tidier

1) A power tells you how many times a number is multiplied by itself.

2) Powers are written like this:

> 2^7 means 'two to the power 7' $= 2 \times 2 \times 2 \times 2 \times 2 \times 2 \times 2$
>
> 6^5 means 'six to the power 5' $= 6 \times 6 \times 6 \times 6 \times 6$
>
> 7^2 means 'seven to the power 2' or '7 squared' $= 7 \times 7$
>
> 4^3 means 'four to the power 3' or '4 cubed' $= 4 \times 4 \times 4$

There are 7 lots of 2 multiplied together.

See page 13 for more on square and cube numbers.

Letters Can Be Multiplied Together

1) ALGEBRA is using letters to stand for numbers.

2) Sometimes we use a letter because we don't know the number.

3) Sometimes we use a letter to stand for any number.

4) Either way, you can usually treat the letters as if they were numbers.

5) With algebra, there are a few rules which tell you how to make things look a bit simpler:

LEAVE OUT '×' SIGNS BETWEEN LETTERS:

* 'abc' means 'a×b×c'.
* Write '2 × n' as just '2n'.
* Write numbers before letters, so 'g × 4' is '4g' NOT 'g4'.

LETTERS CAN HAVE POWERS TOO:

* 'a^4' means '$a \times a \times a \times a$'
* 'gn^2' means 'g×n×n'. (Note that only the n is squared, not the g as well).

BRACKETS CAN HELP LUMP BITS TOGETHER:

* '$(gn)^2$' means 'g×g×n×n'. The ^{2} is outside the brackets so BOTH letters are squared.
* '$(q - r)^2$' means '$(q - r) \times (q - r)$'.
* '-3^2' means $-(3 \times 3) = -9$, BUT $(-3)^2$ means $-3 \times -3 = 9$.

When we tidy things up like this it's called simplifying.

"I've got the power! oh, oh, oh, oh..." Oh no, I'm feeling kinda 90s...

I hope all that algebra stuff hasn't put you off. It makes life simpler for maths teachers, but it can seem pretty scary for the rest of us. Learn this page, then try simplifying these using the rules:

1) a) $3 \times 3 \times 3 \times 3$ b) $4 \times 4 \times 4$ c) $a \times a \times a \times a \times a$ d) $3 \times a \times b \times b$ e) $b \times b \times 7$

Square Roots

Take a deep breath, and get ready for this page. Good luck with it, I'll be <u>rootin'</u> for ya...

Square Roots

1) '<u>Squared</u>' means '<u>times by itself</u>' : $P^2 = P \times P$.

2) <u>SQUARE ROOT</u> is the <u>reverse</u> of this:

> <u>'Square Root' means</u>
> <u>'What Number Times by Itself gives...'</u>

<u>EXAMPLE 1</u>: Find the square root of 49 (written as 'find $\sqrt{49}$')
To do this you should say "what number times by itself gives... 49?".
$7 \times 7 = 49$, so $\sqrt{49} = \underline{7}$.

<u>EXAMPLE 2</u>: Find $\sqrt{100}$
Say "what number times by itself gives... 100?".
$10 \times 10 = 100$, so $\sqrt{100} = \underline{10}$.

It will help <u>a lot</u> if you know the square numbers off by heart — see page 13.

> You can find square roots on your <u>calculator</u>
> using the <u>SQUARE ROOT BUTTON</u>: E.g. press 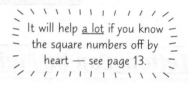 <u>7</u>

If you're not sure what buttons do what on your calculator — have a look at page 3.

Square Roots can be Positive or Negative

1) When you take the square root of a number, the answer can actually be <u>positive</u> or <u>negative</u>.

2) You always have a positive and negative version of the <u>same number</u>.

E.g. The square roots of 4 are $+\sqrt{4}$ and $-\sqrt{4}$, which are equal to +2 and −2

3) To understand why, try <u>squaring both +2 and −2</u>:

$$2^2 = 2 \times 2 = 4 \quad \text{but also} \quad (-2)^2 = (-2) \times (-2) = 4$$

4) Your <u>calculator</u> will <u>only</u> give you the <u>POSITIVE</u> square root.
It's up to you to <u>REMEMBER</u> to give the <u>negative one as well</u>.

Doh!

Cube Roots

Just like square rooting is the <u>reverse</u> of squaring, <u>cube rooting</u> is the reverse of... <u>cubing</u>.

Cube Roots

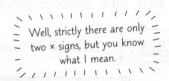

Well, strictly there are only two × signs, but you know what I mean.

1) '<u>Cubed</u>' means '<u>times by itself three times</u>' : $T^3 = T \times T \times T$.

2) <u>CUBE ROOT</u> is the <u>reverse</u> of this:

> ### 'Cube Root' means 'What Number Times by Itself THREE TIMES gives...'

3) Unlike square roots, there's only ever <u>one answer</u> for cube roots.

Cube roots of <u>positive numbers</u> are always <u>POSITIVE</u>.

Cube roots of <u>negative numbers</u> are always <u>NEGATIVE</u>.

Notice the little 3.

EXAMPLE: <u>Find the cube root of 64</u> (written as 'find $\sqrt[3]{64}$')

You should say "What number times by itself three times gives... 64?"

This is not always as obvious as for square roots, so take a few guesses:

> Try $3^3 = 3 \times 3 \times 3 = 27$ (Too small...)
>
> Try $5^3 = 5 \times 5 \times 5 = 125$ (Too big...)
>
> Try $4^3 = 4 \times 4 \times 4 = \underline{64}$ (Just right!)

So if $4^3 = 64$, then the answer is $\sqrt[3]{64} = \underline{4}$.

The number is <u>positive</u>, so the cube root is <u>positive too</u>.

> On your calculator you can use the <u>cube root button</u> (if it has one):
> Press $\sqrt[3]{}$ 64 = $\underline{4}$

"Cue brute" — that's what they call me when I play snooker...

<u>LEARN</u> the last <u>2 pages</u> with all the <u>methods for finding square roots and cube roots</u>.
Then give these questions a go:

1) a) If $g^2 = 36$, write down both answers for g (i.e. find $+\sqrt{36}$ and $-\sqrt{36}$).
   b) If $b^3 = 27$, find b ($\sqrt[3]{27}$).

2) Use your calculator to find: a) $\sqrt{200}$ b) $\sqrt[3]{8000}$

For a) what is the other square root of 200 that your calculator didn't give?

Algebra — Simplifying

Algebra really scares so many people. But honestly, it's not that bad. You've just got to make sure you <u>understand and learn</u> these <u>basic rules</u> for dealing with algebra. After that, all it needs is practice, practice, practice... and a little love.

Terms

You need to understand what a <u>TERM</u> is:

1) <u>A TERM IS A GROUP OF NUMBERS, LETTERS AND BRACKETS, ALL MULTIPLIED OR DIVIDED TOGETHER.</u>

2) Terms are <u>SEPARATED BY + AND − SIGNS</u>   e.g. $4x^2 - 3py - 5 + 3p$

<u>Four different terms.</u>

3) Terms always have a + or − <u>ATTACHED TO THE FRONT OF THEM.</u>

4) e.g.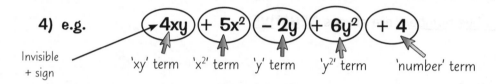

Invisible + sign

'xy' term   'x² term   'y' term   'y² term   'number' term

5) When terms are <u>grouped together</u> like this, it's called an <u>EXPRESSION</u>.

Like... Yeah love. I err... collect like terms err... and stuff...

This date isn't going well...

Simplify Expressions By Collecting Like Terms

1) To <u>simplify</u> an expression, <u>collect together</u> all the terms that have the <u>same letter</u> or <u>group of letters</u> in them — called '<u>LIKE TERMS</u>'.

2) <u>Numbers on their own</u> are 'like terms' because they all have '<u>no letters</u>' in.

EXAMPLE: Simplify the expression: $2x - 4 + 5x + 6$

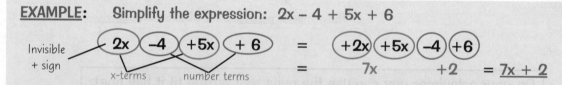

Invisible + sign

x-terms   number terms

$= \quad 7x \qquad +2 \quad = \underline{7x + 2}$

1) <u>Put bubbles round each term</u> — including the <u>+/− sign</u> IN FRONT of each.

2) <u>Move the bubbles</u> so that <u>LIKE TERMS are together</u>.

3) <u>Combine LIKE TERMS</u> by adding or subtracting.
   So $2x + 5x = \underbrace{x + x}_{\text{2 lots of x}} + \underbrace{x + x + x + x + x}_{\text{5 lots of x}} = \underbrace{7x}_{\text{7 lots of x}}$.   **AND** $-4 + 6 = \underline{+2}$.
   (Use a number line to help — p.84)

4) So $2x - 4 + 5x + 6$ simplifies to: $\underline{7x + 2}$.

Algebra — Brackets

Multiplying Out Brackets

We use brackets with numbers to say which part of a calculation should be done first (see p. 3).

It's a bit different with algebra — you're often asked to 'MULTIPLY OUT' or 'EXPAND' an expression with a bracket in. Here's how:

> To EXPAND a bracket, multiply the bit on the outside with everything on the inside.

EXAMPLE 1: Expand $3(2x + 5)$

This means $3 \times (2x + 5)$, so multiply the '2x' by 3, and the '+5' by 3 too:

$$3(2x + 5) = 6x + 15$$
$$3 \times 2x \qquad 3 \times 5$$

LEARN THESE THREE RULES:

1) When letters are multiplied together, they are written next to each other, e.g. $p \times q = pq$.
2) $R \times R = R^2$, and TY^2 means $T \times Y \times Y$, but $(TY)^2$ means $T \times T \times Y \times Y$.
3) A minus outside the bracket REVERSES ALL THE SIGNS when you multiply.

EXAMPLE 2: $4p(3r - 2t) = 12pr - 8pt$
$$4p \times 3r \qquad 4p \times -2t$$

EXAMPLE 3: $-4(3p - 7q) = -12p + 28q$ — Note both signs have been reversed — Rule 3.
The +3p became −12p, and the −7q became +28q.
$$-4 \times 3p \qquad -4 \times -7q$$

1) You can also be asked to FACTORISE an expression — this means putting brackets back in.
2) To factorise, look at what will go into both terms and put this outside a bracket.

E.g. factorise the expression $5a + 10$:
5 will go into both terms so put 5(   ).
Then find something to go inside the bracket that will make 5a + 10 when you multiply it out:
$5(a + 2)$ multiplies out to give 5a + 10, so $5a + 10 = 5(a + 2)$.

Go forth and multiply out brackets...

Learn all the key facts on the last 2 pages, then have a go at these questions to see if you've got it.
1) Simplify: a) $5x + 3y - 4 - 2y - x$ b) $3x + 2 + 5xy + 6x - 7$
2) Expand: a) $2(x - 2)$ b) $x(5 + x)$ c) $y(y + x)$ d) $3y(2x - 6)$

Number Patterns and Sequences

With number patterns, you need to be able to work out the rule for getting the next number in the sequence. There are five different types that you need to be able to find the rule for.

FINDING THE RULE FOR EXTENDING THE PATTERN MEANS...

WORK OUT WHAT YOU DO TO THE PREVIOUS TERM TO GET TO THE NEXT TERM

1) 'Add or Subtract the Same Number'

The SECRET is to WRITE THE DIFFERENCES IN THE GAPS between each pair of numbers:

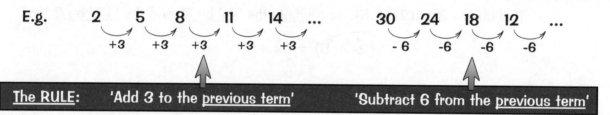

E.g. 2   5   8   11   14   ...   30   24   18   12   ...
       +3   +3   +3   +3   +3   -6   -6   -6   -6

The RULE: 'Add 3 to the previous term'   'Subtract 6 from the previous term'

2) 'Add or Subtract a Changing Number'

Again, WRITE THE CHANGE IN THE GAPS, as shown here:

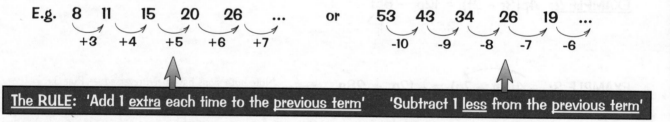

E.g. 8   11   15   20   26   ...   or   53   43   34   26   19   ...
      +3   +4   +5   +6   +7   -10   -9   -8   -7   -6

The RULE: 'Add 1 extra each time to the previous term'   'Subtract 1 less from the previous term'

3) Multiply by the Same Number Each Time

This type has the same number MULTIPLYING the previous number in the pattern each time:

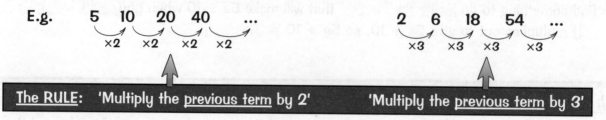

E.g.   5   10   20   40   ...   2   6   18   54   ...
         ×2   ×2   ×2   ×2   ×3   ×3   ×3   ×3

The RULE: 'Multiply the previous term by 2'   'Multiply the previous term by 3'

Number Patterns and Sequences

Just <u>two more</u> patterns to go...

4) <u>Divide by the Same Number Each Time</u>

This type have the same number <u>DIVIDING</u> the previous number each time:

E.g.

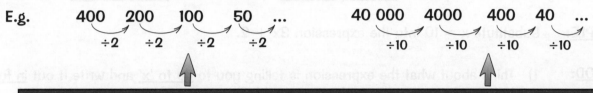

| The RULE: | 'Divide the <u>previous term</u> by 2' | 'Divide the <u>previous term</u> by 10' |

5) <u>Add the Previous Two Terms</u>

This type of sequence works by <u>ADDING THE LAST TWO NUMBERS</u> to get the next one.

E.g.   1   1   2   3   5   8   13 ...   2   4   6   10   16 ...

1+1 1+2 2+3 3+5 5+8 8+13   2+4 4+6 6+10 10+16

| The RULE: | 'Add the <u>previous two terms</u>' |

This sequence is a pretty special one known
as the <u>FIBONACCI SEQUENCE</u>.
You don't need to know that for your
exam, but if you're ever on a game show
and it's the £1 000 000 question,
be sure to look me up and thank me.

"LEARN THIS PAGE, LEARN THIS PAGE..." — I can see a pattern here...

The <u>first thing</u> to do when faced with a sequence is to work out the <u>differences</u> between the numbers.
If that doesn't help, check if they're being <u>multiplied</u> or <u>divided</u> by a number instead.
If that still fails, try <u>adding together</u> two numbers next to each other and see if you come out with the
next one in the sequence. You might also be asked to <u>carry on</u> the sequence <u>using the rule</u>.
Learn the last 2 pages, then write down the rules and find the next number in the pattern for these:
1) a) 21 19 17 15 13 11 ...   b) 1 2 4 7 11 16 ...   c) 2 20 200 2000 20 000 ...
2) a) 64 32 16 8 4 2 ...   b) 9 10 19 29 48 77 ...

Formulas

A <u>formula</u> is a way of giving instructions <u>without</u> using loads of <u>words</u>.
So instead of saying "Square a number, times it by 7 and take away 11", say $N = 7x^2 - 11$. <u>Nice</u>.

Substitution — Putting Numbers In

Algebra uses <u>letters in place of numbers</u>.
Sometimes you're asked to put the <u>numbers</u> <u>BACK IN</u> — this is called <u>SUBSTITUTION</u>.

<u>EXAMPLE</u>:   Substitute $x = 10$ into the expression $3x + 2$.

<u>METHOD</u>:
1) Think about what the expression is telling you to <u>do to 'x'</u> and write it out <u>in full</u>.
   Here we have to <u>times 'x' by 3</u> and <u>add 2</u>: $3 \times x + 2$.

2) Put the number <u>in place</u> of the letter.
   Here, $x = 10$, so: $3 \times 10 + 2$.

3) Finally, work out the <u>value</u>: $3 \times 10 + 2 = 30 + 2 = \underline{32}$.

> Use BODMAS (p. 3) to work things out in the right order.

When Using Formulas, Do One Bit at a Time...

Substituting numbers into <u>formulas</u> is just the same.
They might look tricky, but take it <u>step by step</u>.

Example:	Temperature can be measured in <u>degrees Celsius</u> (°C) or <u>degrees Fahrenheit</u> (°F).

We can use the <u>formula</u>: $F = \dfrac{9}{5}C + 32$ to <u>swap</u> between the two.

If the temperature is 15 °C (<u>C = 15</u>), find the temperature in <u>Fahrenheit (F)</u>.

Method:

1) <u>Write out the formula in full</u> $F = \dfrac{9}{5} \times C + 32$

2) <u>Write it again</u>, but put numbers in place of any letters you know.
   Here you're told that $C = 15$. $F = \dfrac{9}{5} \times 15 + 32$

3) Work it out <u>IN STAGES</u>.
   <u>WRITE DOWN</u> values for each bit <u>as you go along</u>.
   $F = 27 + 32$
   $F = 59$
   $\underline{F = 59°}$

There's no substitute for a bit of hard work I'm afraid...

There's no getting out of it, you'll have to <u>learn everything on this page</u>. Then have a crack at these:

1) Substitute $x = 2$ into these expressions: a) $5x + 15$ b) $10x - 7$ c) $\dfrac{1}{2}x + 4$
2) Use the formula $A = 2C - 6$ to find A, when $C = 9$

Making Formulas from Words

You need to know the "tricks of the trade" for making formulas from words.
There are two main types:

Type 1:

Where you have instructions about what to do with a number and you have to write it as a formula.
The instructions can be any one of these (where 'x' stands for a number):

> 1) Multiply x   2) Divide x   3) Square or square root x (x^2 or $\sqrt{x}$)
>
> 4) Cube x (x^3)   5) Add or subtract a number

Example 1:   "To find y, subtract four from x"

Answer: Start with x   →   x – 4   so $y = x - 4$
$$\text{Subtract 4}$$

Example 2:   "To find y, divide x by three and then subtract seven.
Write a formula for y."

Answer: Start with x   → $\dfrac{x}{3}$ → $\dfrac{x}{3} - 7$ So $y = \dfrac{x}{3} - 7$
$$\text{Divide it by 3} \qquad \text{Subtract 7}$$

Type 2:

Where you have to make up a formula by putting in letters
like 'C' for 'cost' or 'n' for 'number of something-or-others'.

Example: 'CHOCCO-BURGERS' cost 58 pence each. Write a formula for the
total cost, T, of buying n 'CHOCCO-BURGERS' at 58p each.

Answer: T stands for the total cost

n stands for the number of 'CHOCCO-BURGERS'

In WORDS the formula is: Total Cost = Number of 'CHOCCO-BURGERS' × 58p
Putting the LETTERS in: T = n × 58   or to write it better: T = 58n

I love this page SO MUCH that words fail me...

Nope. I got nothin'. Best just do these questions:

1) y is found by multiplying x by five and then subtracting three.
Write down a formula for y in terms of x.

2) Reindeer kebabs cost 95p each.
Write a formula for the total cost, C pence, of buying n kebabs.

Solving Equations

The 'proper' way to solve equations is shown on the next page.
The 'proper' way can sometimes be hard though — so there are some easier methods shown below.
The problem with these is that you can't always use them on very tricky equations.
In most exam questions though, they do just fine.

1) The 'Common Sense' Way

1) The unknown 'x' is just a number.
2) The 'equation' is just a clue to help you find out what the number is.

Example: "Solve this equation: $3x + 4 = 46$"
(i.e. find what number x is)

Answer: This is what you should say to yourself:

"Something + 4 = 46"   hmm, so that 'something' must be **42**. 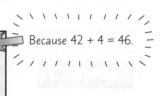 Because 42 + 4 = 46.

So that means $3x = 42$, which means '3 times something = 42'.

So it must be $42 \div 3$ which is 14 so $\underline{x = 14}$.

And doing a final check gives $3 \times 14 + 4 = \underline{46}$, so it must be right.

2) The Trial and Error Way

1) This works best if the answer is a whole number.
2) In the trial and error method, you find a number that's too big, and a number that's too small, and then try values in between them.

Example: "Solve for x: $3x + 5 = 11$"
(i.e. find out what number x is)

Answer:
Try x = 1: $(3 \times 1) + 5 = 3 + 5 = 8$ — no good, it's too small (we want 11)
Try x = 3: $(3 \times 3) + 5 = 9 + 5 = 14$ — no good, it's too big

SO TRY IN BETWEEN: x = 2: $(3 \times 2) + 5 = 6 + 5 = 11$,   YES, so $\underline{x = 2}$.

But I'm innocent your honour — this trial is an error...

~~Loan those two methods.~~ No. ~~Learn these to meatheads.~~ No. Learn these two methods. Splendid.
Now use either one of them to answer these:
1) Solve: $4x + 12 = 20$ 2) Solve: $5x - 9 = 6$

Solving Equations

The 'proper' way of solving equations isn't too difficult, it just needs <u>lots of practice</u>.

3) The 'Proper' Way

> ### GOLDEN RULES FOR SOLVING EQUATIONS
> 1) Always do the <u>SAME THING</u> to <u>both sides of the equation</u>.
> 2) To get rid of something, do the <u>opposite</u>.
>   The opposite of $+$ is $-$ and the opposite of $-$ is $+$.
>   The opposite of $\times$ is $\div$ and the opposite of $\div$ is $\times$.
> 3) Keep going until you have a letter <u>on its own</u>.

Example 1: Solve $5x = 15$

$$5x = 15$$
$$x = 15 \div 5$$
$$\underline{x = 3}$$

$5x$ means $5 \times x$, so do the opposite — <u>divide</u> both sides by 5.

Example 2: Solve $\dfrac{p}{3} = 2$

$$\frac{p}{3} = 2$$
$$p = 2 \times 3$$
$$\underline{p = 6}$$

$\dfrac{p}{3}$ means $p \div 3$, so do the opposite — <u>multiply</u> both sides by 3.

Example 3: Solve $4y - 3 = 17$

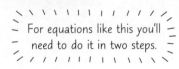

$$4y - 3 = 17$$
$$4y = 20$$
$$\underline{y = 5}$$

For equations like this you'll need to do it in two steps.

1) The opposite of -3 is $+3$ — so <u>add</u> 3 to both sides.
2) The opposite of $\times 4$ is $\div 4$ — so <u>divide</u> both sides by 4.

Example 4: Solve $2(x + 3) = 11$

For questions with brackets you might have to use three steps.

$$2(x + 3) = 11$$
$$2x + 6 = 11$$
$$2x = 5$$
$$\underline{x = 2.5}$$

1) <u>Multiply out the brackets</u> (p. 89). Now you can solve it like Example 3.
2) The opposite of $+6$ is -6 — so <u>subtract</u> 6 from both sides.
3) The opposite of $\times 2$ is $\div 2$ — so <u>divide</u> both sides by 2.

This page could solve all your algebra problems...

If you can solve equations the '<u>proper</u>' way then you might as well get good at it.
This way you'll be able to solve <u>any equation</u> on the exam, instead of just hoping you get an easy one...

1) Solve these equations: a) $3x = 18$ b) $\dfrac{q}{4} = 8$ c) $3x + 1 = 13$ d) $5(y + 2) = 20$

Revision Test for Section Seven

1) Work out: a) -3×-2 b) -4×8 c) $12 \div -4$ d) $-20 \div -4$

2) Work out the value of: a) 6^3 b) 7^2 c) 4^4

3) Simplify: a) $4 \times n \times n \times n$ b) $a \times a \times 2$

4) Find all possible answers of: a) The square root of 256   b) $\sqrt[3]{216}$.

5) Simplify the expression: $3x + 4y + 2x - y$ ⟵ Don't forget to look for any invisible + signs.

6) Expand these expressions: a) $4(3g + 5h - 1)$ b) $x(x - 6)$

7) Find the next two terms in these sequences of numbers:
   a) 3, 7, 11, 15, ..., ...   b) 36, 28, 21, 15, 10, ..., ...
   c) 3, 6, 12, 24, ... , ...   d) 1200, 600, 300, ..., ...
   e) 2, 5, 7, 12, 19, ..., ...
   For each sequence, say what the rule is for extending the pattern.

8) Ellen's thermometer only measures in Celsius (°C) but her dad can only understand temperatures in Fahrenheit (°F). She knows that to get a temperature in °F you need to 'times the temperature in °C by $\frac{9}{5}$ and then add 32'.

   a) Write out a formula for changing °C into °F.
   b) Use your formula to find the temperature in Fahrenheit when it is 30 °C.

   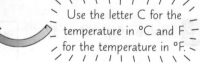 Use the letter C for the temperature in °C and F for the temperature in °F.

9) 'To find y, you double x and add 4.' Write this as a formula.

10) Write a formula to find the number of miles (M) you cover on a car journey lasting H hours, if you travel 40 miles every hour.

11) Find x if $x^2 = 81$. (Use trial and error.)

12) Solve these equations:
    a) $x + 3 = 7$
    b) $4x = 28$
    c) $2x - 12 = 6$
    d) $5(x + 5) = 10$

Answers

Section One

P.6 Ordering Numbers:
1) **a)** One million, two hundred and thirty-four thousand, five hundred and thirty-one
   b) Twenty-three thousand, four hundred and fifty-six **c)** Two thousand, four hundred and fifteen
   d) Three thousand, four hundred and two **e)** Two hundred and three thousand, four hundred and twelve
2) 56 421 **3)** 9, 23, 87, 345, 493, 1029, 3004 **4)** 0.008, 0.09, 0.1, 0.2, 0.307, 0.37

P.7 Addition and Subtraction: **1) a)** 806 **b)** 186 **2) a)** 171 cm **b)** 19 cm

P.8 Adding and Subtracting Decimals: **1) a)** £2.84 **b)** £2.16

P.9 Multiplying by 10, 100, etc: **1) a)** 3450 **b)** 1230 **c)** 9650 **d)** 180 000

P.10 Dividing by 10, 100, etc: **1) a)** 0.245 **b)** 6.542 **c)** 0.00308 **d)** 1.6

P.12 Dividing Without a Calculator: **1)** 336 **2)** 616 **3)** 832 **4)** 17 976 **5)** 121 **6)** 12 **7)** 12 **8)** 25

P.14 Special Number Sequences:
1) EVENS: 2, 4, 6, 8, 10, 12, 14, 16, 18, 20
   ODDS: 1, 3, 5, 7, 9, 11, 13, 15, 17, 19
   SQUARES: 1, 4, 9, 16, 25, 36, 49, 64, 81, 100
   CUBES: 1, 8, 27, 64, 125, 216, 343, 512, 729, 1000
   POWERS OF 2: 2, 4, 8, 16, 32, 64, 128, 256, 512, 1024
   POWERS OF 10: 10, 100, 1000, 10 000, 100 000, 1 000 000, 10 000 000,
                 100 000 000, 1 000 000 000, 10 000 000 000
   TRIANGLE Nos: 1, 3, 6, 10, 15, 21, 28, 36, 45, 55
2) **a)** 56, 134, 156, 36, 64 **b)** 23, 45, 81, 25, 97, 125 **c)** 81, 25, 36, 64 **d)** 125, 64 **e)** 64 **f)** 45, 36

P.15 Multiples, Factors and Primes:
1) 6, 12, 18, 24, 30, 36, 42, 48, 54, 60 and 7, 14, 21, 28, 35, 42, 49, 56, 63, 70
2) 1, 2, 3, 4, 6, 9, 12, 18, 36
3) 2, 3, 5, 7, 11, 13, 17, 19, 23, 29

P.16 Fractions, Decimals and Percentages: **1) a)** 7/10 and 70% **b)** 1/100 and 1% **c)** 6/10 = 3/5 and 60%

P.17 Fractions: **1) a)** 5/6 **b)** 2/3 **2)** 2/3

P.18 Fractions: **1) a)** 15/24 = 5/8 **b)** 32/35 **c)** 4/8 = 1/2 **d)** 2/5 **e)** 7/10

P.19 Ratios: **1)** 40p **2)** £500:£700

Revision Test for Section One

<u>1)</u> One million, three hundred and six thousand, five hundred and fifteen.
<u>2)</u> **a)** 2, 23, 45, 123, 132, 789, 2200, 6534 **b)** 0.0021, 0.003, 0.01, 0.05, 0.12, 0.6
<u>3)</u> **a)** 1145 **b)** 165 **c)** 11.13   <u>4)</u> **a)** £7.79 **b)** £2.21   <u>5)</u> £120   <u>6)</u> 32p   <u>7)</u> **a)** 759 **b)** 29
<u>8)</u> Square numbers are what you get when you multiply a number by itself, they are the areas of squares of side lengths
   1, 2, 3, etc. The first five are: 1, 4, 9, 16, 25.   <u>9)</u> 1, 2, 3, 5, 6, 10, 15, 30   <u>10)</u> **a)** 0.6 **b)** 6/10 = 3/5
<u>11)</u> 1/4   <u>12)</u> 7/8   <u>13)</u> **a)** 4/15 **b)** 15/48 = 5/16 **c)** 7/8 **d)** 2/7   <u>14)</u> £200:£600   <u>15)</u> **a)** £15 **b)** £315

Section Two

P.23 Symmetry and Tessellations:
H : 2 lines of symmetry, rotational symmetry order 2,   **Z :** 0 lines of symmetry, rotational symmetry order 2,
T : 1 line of symmetry, rotational symmetry order 1,   **N :** 0 lines of symmetry, rotational symmetry order 2,
E : 1 line of symmetry, rotational symmetry order 1,   **✗ :** 4 lines of symmetry, rotational symmetry order 4,
P.27 Regular Polygons:
1) A regular polygon is a many-sided shape where all the sides and angles are the same.
2) Equilateral triangle, square, regular pentagon, regular hexagon, regular heptagon, regular octagon

P.28 Perimeters: **1)** Perimeter is the distance all the way around the outside of a shape.   **2)** 42 cm

P.29 Areas: **1)** 40 cm^2 **2)** 20 cm^2

P.31 Volume: **1)** 9 m^3

P.32 Congruence and Similarity: **1) a)** i, ii and iv are similar.   **b)** i and ii are congruent.

Answers

Revision Test for Section Two

1) a) 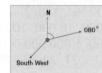 b) c)

2) a) order 2   b) order 1   c) order 6   3) a) 4 cm   b) They're the same size.
4) rhombus   5) See page 26. The triangular prism and the cylinder are prisms.
6) 8 sides, all the same length, 8 lines of symmetry, rotational symmetry order 8, all angles the same.
7) a) 3 m   b) 32 m   8) 84 m²   9) a) 18 cm²   b) 36 cm²   10) a) 6 m   b) 3.142 or 3
11) 37.7 cm   12) 5500 cm³   13) See page 32.

Section Three

P.34 Metric and Imperial Units: 1) a) 200   b) 650   2) a) 2   b) 3   3) 4
P.36 Conversion Factors: 1) 160 kg   2) 2 pounds (lbs)
P.37 Rounding Off: 1) a) 3   b) 5   c) 2   d) 7   e) 3   2) a) 300   b) 500   c) 100   3) a) 5.4   b) 0.1
P.38 Clock Time Questions: 1) 5.15 pm 2) 1440 ; 86 400 3) 3hrs 30 min; 5hrs 45 min 4) 4.05 pm
P.39 Compass Directions and Bearings: 1) a) and b) See right.
P.41 Maps and Map Scales: 1) 1400 m   2) 3 cm
P.42 Maps and Directions: 1) C1   2) South-East   3) The School

Revision Test for Section Three

1) a) 60 mm b) 0.06 m   2) Yes   3) The blanket   4) £200
5) a) 1   b) 3   c) 16   d) 12   6) a) 250 b) 900   7) a) 5.3 b) 3.5   c) 6.2 8) 12.50 pm
9) a) 21.25 b) 9.25 pm   10) See page 39   11) See right   12) 360 km
13) 12 cm   14) 0.01 m/s   15) a) 3 hours b) 13.18 or 1.18 pm

Section Four

P.46 Lines and Angles: 1) Actual angles given — accept answers within 10°:
a) 36° b) 79° c) 162° d) 287°

P.47 Measuring Angles with Protractors: 2) See above, answers to P.46.
P.50 Parallel and Perpendicular Lines: See right.
P.54 The Four Transformations — Reflection:
1) A to B rotation ¼ turn (90°) clockwise about the origin (0,0).
   B to C reflection in the line y = x.   C to A reflection in the y-axis (line x = 0).
   A to D translation of 9 left and 7 down.
P.56 Constructing Triangles: 1) Measure all sides to check it's right.   2) BC = 6 cm

Revision Test for Section Four

1) a) Acute b) Right angle c) Obtuse d) Acute   2) a) 68° b) 27° c) 270° d) 223°   3) 160°
4) X = 110°, Y = 40°   5) a) 100° b) Corresponding angles
6) a) Rotation ¼ turn (90°) anticlockwise about the origin (0,0)   b) Reflection in the x-axis (line y = 0)
   c) Enlargement scale factor 2 with centre (2,6)   7) Measure all sides to check it's right.

Answers

Section Five

P.58 Probability: 1) a) likely **b)** $\frac{1}{4}$ (or 25% or 0.25)

P.59 Equal and Unequal Probabilities: 1) $\frac{1}{5}$ or 20% or 0.2

P.60 Listing Outcomes: 1) See right. **a)** 36 **b)** 5 **c)** P(8) = $\frac{5}{36}$

P.61 Types of Data: 1) a) discrete **b)** qualitative **c)** qualitative **d)** continuous

P.63 Questionnaires: 1) a) "A lot of television" can mean different things to different people. **b)** This is a leading question.
c) The answers to this question do not cover all the possible options.

P.65 Mean, Median, Mode and Range:
First, order the numbers: -14, -12, -5, -5, 0, 1, 3, 6, 7, 8, 10, 14, 18, 23, 25
Mean = 5.27,   Median = 6,   Mode = -5,   Range = 39

P.71 Bar Charts: 1) See bar chart on the right.

P.73 Pie Charts: See pie chart below.

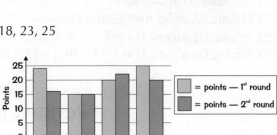

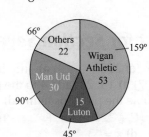

Revision Test for Section Five

1) P(not 6) = 0.8   **2)** 20%   **3) a)** See right **b)** $\frac{1}{12}$

4) a) primary **b)** quantitative **c)** discrete

5) He could take a sample, and put the data into groups / classes.

6) It's not clear what he means by "big", and also people might be too embarrassed to answer truthfully / it could be a sensitive question.

7) First put in order: 2, 3, 4, 6, 7, 7, 12, 15 **a)** 7 **b)** 6.5 **c)** 7 **d)** 13

8) Pictogram, 35 angry customers.   **9)** No, the graph shows no correlation.

10) a) Angles are: Blue 108°, Red 135°, Yellow 36°, White 81°.
b) See pie chart to the right.

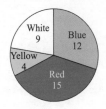

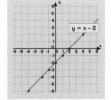

Section Six

P.75 X and Y Coordinates:
1) A(4, 5)   B(6, 0)   C(5, -5)   D(0, -3)   E(-5, -2)   F(-4, 0)   G(-3, 3)   H(0, 5)

P.76 Midpoint of a Line Segment: 1) (3, 5)

P.79 Straight-Line Graphs: 1) and **2)** See right.

x	-4	-2	-1	0	1	2	4
y	-6	-4	-3	-2	-1	0	2

Revision Test for Section Six

1) a) yes **b)** yes   **2)** See far right

3) (-2, 3)

4) a) 2 **b)** 4 **c)** 3 **d)** 1

5) a)

x	-5	-3	-1	0	1	2	4	6
y	-2	0	2	3	4	5	7	9

b)

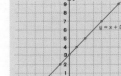

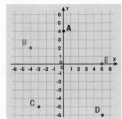

6) a) walking 1.5 km away at a steady speed
b) stopped **c)** 2.5 km

7) a) 5 sheep **b)** 30 chickens

Answers

Section Seven

P.84 Negative Numbers: **1) a)** +12   **b)** -6   **c)** -3   **d)** +1

P.85 Powers and Letters: **1) a)** 3^4 **b)** 4^3 **c)** a^5 **d)** $3ab^2$ **e)** $7b^2$

P.87 Cube Roots: **1) a)** +6 and –6   **b)** 3   **2) a)** 14.1421... (and other answer is –14.1421...)   **b)** 20

P.89 Algebra — Brackets: **1) a)** $4x + y – 4$ **b)** $9x + 5xy – 5$ **2) a)** $2x – 4$ **b)** $5x + x^2$ **c)** $y^2 + xy$ **d)** $6xy – 18y$

P.91 Number Patterns and Sequences: **1) a)** 9 (subtract 2 from the previous term)
b) 22 (add one extra each time to the previous term)   **c)** 200 000 (multiply the previous term by 10)
2) a) 1 (divide the previous term by 2)   **b)** 125 (add the previous two terms)

P.92 Formulas: **1) a)** 25   **b)** 13   **c)** 5   **2)** A = 12

P.93 Making Formulas from Words: **1)** $y = 5x – 3$ **2)** C = 95n

P.94 Solving Equations: **1)** x = 2   **2)** x = 3

P.95 Solving Equations: **1) a)** x = 6   **b)** q = 32   **c)** x = 4   **d)** y = 2

Revision Test for Section Seven

1) **a)** +6   **b)** –32   **c)** –3   **d)** +5   **2) a)** 216   **b)** 49   **c)** 256   **3) a)** $4n^3$ **b)** $2a^2$ **4) a)** +16, –16   **b)** 6
5) $5x + 3y$ **6) a)** $12g + 20h – 4$ **b)** $x^2 – 6x$ **7) a)** 19, 23; add 4 to the previous term   **b)** 6, 3; subtract one
less each time from the previous term   **c)** 48, 96; double the previous term   **d)** 150, 75; halve the previous term
e) 31, 50; add the previous two terms   **8) a)** $F = \frac{9}{5}C + 32$ **b)** 86 ºF   **9)** $y = 2x + 4$ **10)** M = 40H
11) x = +9 or –9   **12) a)** x = 4   **b)** x = 7   **c)** x = 9   **d)** x = –3

Index

Index